CAMBRIDGE LIBRARY COLLECTION

Books of enduring scholarly value

History

The books reissued in this series include accounts of historical events and movements by eye-witnesses and contemporaries, as well as landmark studies that assembled significant source materials or developed new historiographical methods. The series includes work in social, political and military history on a wide range of periods and regions, giving modern scholars ready access to influential publications of the past.

A Complete Account of the Settlement at Port Jackson, in New South Wales

In May 1787 a fleet of ships carrying convicts left England bound for Botany Bay, New South Wales, where they were to establish a settlement. One of the crew on board the *Charlotte* was Watkin Tench (c.1758–1833), who wrote about the voyage of what was later known as the First Fleet. He remained in New South Wales, living in Port Jackson (part of present-day Sydney) from 1788 to 1791, and in this work, published in 1793, he gives a vivid, first-hand account of the early years of British settlement. The chapters are chronologically organised and discuss the many challenges settlers in the fledgling colony faced in staying alive, such as illness and lack of food and other provisions. He also recounts the often violent encounters and 'unabated animosity' between the settlers and the aboriginal people, making this work an important source on the colonisation of Australia.

T0381645

Cambridge University Press has long been a pioneer in the reissuing of out-of-print titles from its own backlist, producing digital reprints of books that are still sought after by scholars and students but could not be reprinted economically using traditional technology. The Cambridge Library Collection extends this activity to a wider range of books which are still of importance to researchers and professionals, either for the source material they contain, or as landmarks in the history of their academic discipline.

Drawing from the world-renowned collections in the Cambridge University Library, and guided by the advice of experts in each subject area, Cambridge University Press is using state-of-the-art scanning machines in its own Printing House to capture the content of each book selected for inclusion. The files are processed to give a consistently clear, crisp image, and the books finished to the high quality standard for which the Press is recognised around the world. The latest print-on-demand technology ensures that the books will remain available indefinitely, and that orders for single or multiple copies can quickly be supplied.

The Cambridge Library Collection will bring back to life books of enduring scholarly value (including out-of-copyright works originally issued by other publishers) across a wide range of disciplines in the humanities and social sciences and in science and technology.

A Complete Account
of the Settlement
at Port Jackson,
in New South Wales

WATKIN TENCH

CAMBRIDGE
UNIVERSITY PRESS

CAMBRIDGE UNIVERSITY PRESS

Cambridge, New York, Melbourne, Madrid, Cape Town,
Singapore, São Paolo, Delhi, Tokyo, Mexico City

Published in the United States of America by Cambridge University Press, New York

www.cambridge.org
Information on this title: www.cambridge.org/9781108039147

This edition first published 1793
This digitally printed version 2011

ISBN 978-1-108-03914-7 Paperback

A

COMPLETE ACCOUNT

OF THE

SETTLEMENT AT PORT JACKSON,

IN NEW SOUTH WALES,

INCLUDING

AN ACCURATE DESCRIPTION OF THE SITUATION OF THE COLONY;
OF THE NATIVES; AND OF ITS NATURAL PRODUCTIONS:

TAKEN ON THE SPOT,

BY CAPTAIN WATKIN TENCH,

OF THE MARINES.

LONDON:

SOLD BY G NICOL, PALL-MALL; AND J. SEWELL, CORNHILL.

1793.

To Sir WATKIN WILLIAMS WYNN, Bart.

SIR,

A LIFE passed on service, in distant and obscure countries, has hitherto prevented me from aspiring to a personal acquaintance with you. I know you only from the representations of others; not having seen you for the last fourteen years. Consequently I can judge but imperfectly, whether the transactions of a remote and unknown colony will prove sufficiently at‧tractive to engage your attention.

Gratitude to a family, from whom I have received the deepest obligations, nevertheless impels me to beg your acceptance of this tribute.

Descended of illustrious ancestors, and born to a splendid patrimony, the career of manhood opens before you. May your progression in that career, accomplish the hopes which sanguine expectation has formed of your character! Your honourable and revered Father, presents the fairest example.—That like him you may shine incorrupt and independent in the senate; and in private life, practice beneficence without ostentation, and adorn hospitality with elegance, is the earnest and sincere wish of him who has the honour to be,

SIR,

Your most devoted,

and most obedient humble servant,

WATKIN TENCH.

PREFACE.

WHEN it is recollected how much has been written to describe the Settlement of New South Wales, it seems necessary if not to offer an apology, yet to assign a reason, for an additional publication.

The Author embarked in the fleet which sailed to found the establishment at Botany Bay. He shortly after published a Narrative of the Proceedings and State of the Colony, brought up to the beginning of July, 1788, which was well received, and passed through three editions. This could not but inspire both confidence and gratitude; but gratitude, would be badly manifested were he on the presumption of former favour to lay claim to present indulgence. He resumes the subject in the humble hope of communicating information, and increasing knowledge, of the country, which he describes.

He resided at Port Jackson nearly four years: from the 20th of January, 1788, until the 18th of December, 1791. To an active and contemplative mind, a new country is an inexhaustible source of curiosity and speculation. It was the author's custom not only to note daily occurrences, and to inspect and record the progression of improvement; but also, when not prevented by military duties, to penetrate the surrounding country in different directions, in order to examine its nature, and ascertain its relative geographical situations.

The greatest part of the work is inevitably composed of those materials which a journal supplies; but wherever reflections could be introduced without fastidiousness and parade, he has not scrupled to indulge them, in common with every other deviation which the strictness of narrative would allow.

When this publication was nearly ready for the press; and when many of the opinions which it records had been declared, fresh accounts from Port Jackson were received. To the state of a country, where so many anxious trying hours of his life have passed, the author cannot feel indifferent. If by any sudden revolution of the laws of nature; or by any fortunate discovery of those on the spot, it has really become that fertile and prosperous land, which some represent it to be, he begs permission to add his voice to the general congratulation. He rejoices at its success: but it is only justice to himself and those with whom he acted to declare, that they feel no cause of reproach that so complete and happy an alteration did not take place at an earlier period.

CONTENTS.

CONTENTS.

LIST OF SUBSCRIBERS.

A.

Sir Thomas Dyke Ackland, Bart.
Rev. J. Allanson, Malpas
Mrs. Allenborow, Ely
Lt. Adair, Marines
Mr. Anson, Liverpool
Mr. Archer, Mildenhall, Suffolk
Clement Archer, Esq. Conway
Mr. J. Aspinall, Liverpool
Wm. Anderson, Esq. Tower-street
Edward Atherton, Esq. Liverpool
John Atherton, Esq. Prescot
Daniel Ashley, Esq. Frodsham
Major Austin, Royal Gloster Militia
Colonel Averne, Marines

B.

Right Hon. Lord Belgrave, M. P.
Right Hon. Lord Brome, St. John's
    College, Cambridge
Sir Richard Brooke, Bart.
The Hon. Daines Barrington
Tho. Brooke, Esq. M. P.
Mr. Hall, Bartlow, Cambridge
John Blackburne, Esq. M. P.
Col. Basset, North Devon Militia
Capt. Hen. Lidgbird Ball, Royal Navy
Henry Blundell, Esq. Ince (4 copies)
Edw. Brock, Esq. Liverpool
Wm. Bond, Esq. Albion-street, Black
    Friars
Captain Bowen, Royal Navy
Tho. Boycott, Esq. Rudge, Shropshire

Mrs. Boycott
Major Barnston, R. Cheshire Militia
Abraham Ball, Esq. Do.
Tho. L. Brooke, Esq. Do.
Col. Barclay, Marines
Capt. Berkeley, Do.
Capt. Bowater, Do.
Lt. Wm. Bourne, Do.
Lt. Busigny, Do.
Lt. Boys, Do.
R. Bayley, Esq. Stoke, near Plymouth
Benj. Babbage, Esq. Walworth
Wm. Barlow, Esq. Plymouth
Tho. Bridge, Esq. Middlewich
Fran. Bagge, Esq. High Bailiff of the
    Isle of Ely
Rev. James Bentham, A. M. Ely.
Mrs. Barnston, Chester
Mr. S. Barnes, Do.
Mr John Bayley, Do.
Townley Blackwood, Esq. Do.
John Bonner, Esq. Do.
Rev. T. Bancroft, M. A. Do.
S. Broadhurst, Esq. Do.
Mrs. Broadhurst, Do.
Rev. Chancellor Briggs, M. A. Do.
John Buckley, Esq. Do.
Mr. Broster, Do.
Mrs. Bennet, Do.
Rev. R. Baldwin, Harrock, Lancashire
Dr. Brown, Huntingdon
John Biden, Esq. Do.
Henry Burgh, Esq. Stroudwater
Wm. Burgh, Esq. Do.
John Backhouse, Esq. Liverpool

Henry Brown, Esq. Do.
John Barnes, Esq. Thaives Inn
Wm. Bowden, Esq. London
Rich. Bull, Esq.
Mr. Bennet, Emanuel College, Cambridge
Mr. G. A. Bollen, Do.
Mr. Beresford, Do.
Mr. Blackall, Do.
Mr. J. Brooke, Jesus Coll. Cambridge

C.

Right Hon. the Earl of Coventry
Right Hon. the Earl of Carysfort
Lady Carysfort
Rev. H. Cooper, Pembroke Hall, Cambridge
Lady Cooke
Sir Rob. Salisbury Cotton, Bart. M. P. for Cheshire
John Crewe, Esq. M. P. for Do.
Mrs. Crewe
Sir Foster Cunliffe, Bart.
Gov. Campbell, Plymouth Citadel
Bryan Cooke, Esq. Owston, Yorkshire (two copies)
Mrs. Cooke, Do.
Tho. Cholmondeley, Esq. Vale Royal, Cheshire
Rev. George Cotton, L L D. Dean of Chester
Cambridge University Library
Chester Library
Rich. Crop, Esq. Westminster
George Chamberlaine, Esq. Do.
Mrs. Corbet, Hatton, Shropshire
Mrs. Chilton, Liverpool
Rev. Offley Crewe, Muxon, Cheshire

John Culme, Esq. Plymouth
Tho. Cowen, Esq. Do.
John Caneilon, Esq. Threadneedle-st.
George Couch, Esq. Ford
Tho. Corbyn, Esq.
Wm. Croughton, Esq. Friday-street
Miss Collins, London
Mr. Clarke, Plymouth
George Cleather, Esq. Do.
Wm. Cubbin, Esq. Liverpool
Tho. Case, Esq. Red-Hazels, Lancashire
E. Cotton, Esq.
Stapleton Cotton, Esq. 23d Regiment
Mr. Connah, Chester
Clement Courtenay, Esq. Do.
Mrs. Cowper, Overley, Cheshire
Boswell Crewe, Esq. Chester
Wm. Curry, Esq. Eastham, Cheshire
Wm. Currie, Esq. M. D. Chester
Mrs. Comberbatch, Congleton
Miss Comberbatch
Mr. Clay, Liverpool
Rev. G. Chamberlaine, Westminster
Mr. T. C. Clements, Liverpool
Mr. W. Calcott, Do.
Rev. Randal Crewe, Hawarden
Mr. E. Cotton, Trinity-Hall, Camb.
French Chiswell, Esq.
Mr. Cooper
Mrs. Cooper
Mrs. Curzon, Davies-street

D.

Lady Davenport, Bloomsbury-square
P. Whitehall Davies, Esq. Broughton
Miss Davies
Rev. Crewe Davies, Broughton

Col. Duval, Marines
Lieut. G. Drake, Do.
Mrs. Drake, Chester (two copies)
Wm. Dix, Esq. Fron, Flintshire
Mrs. Davenport, Chester
Joseph Dyson, Esq. Chester
P. Dondon, Esq. M. D. Do.
Rev. H. Dillon, B. A. Plymouth
Rich. Dunning, Esq. Do.
J. Davies, Esq. Pay Office, Plymouth
Mr. Wm. Dennison, Liverpool
Mr. Andrew Dodson, Do.
—— Dyer, Esq. South Devon Militia
D. Davenport, Esq. Capestone, Che-
shire
Mrs. Dundas, Barton-court, Bucks
H. Donaldson, Esq. Margaret-street,
Cavendish-square
Mr. Driffield, King's Coll. Cambridge

E.

Rev. Philip Egerton, Oulton, Cheshire
John Egerton, Esq. High Sheriff of
Ditto
Mrs. Egerton, Chester
Rev. J. W. Eyton, Leeswood, Flint-
shire
Mrs. Wynne Eyton
Wm. Elford, Esq. Bickham, Devon
Jonathan Elford, Esq. Plymouth Dock
Mr. Evans, Ely (two copies)
Rev. John Eccles, Lincoln Coll. Ox.
Owen Ellis, Esq. Eyton, Denbighshire
Mr. Ellis, Molesworth, Ely
Mr. Ellis, Chester
J. Evelyn, Esq. Ditto
—— Edwards, Esq. Royal Cheshire
Militia
Edward Elton, Esq. Westminster

F.

—— Fullelove, Esq. London
Leonard Fosbrook, Esq. Chester
Thomas Fluitt, Esq. Ditto
Rich. Fleming, Esq. Ditto
George Foliot, Esq. Ditto
—— Flannagan, Esq. Ditto
Edward Falkner, Esq. Fairfield, Lan-
cashire (two copies)
Mrs. Foliot, Namptwych
Lt. French, Royal Cheshire Militia
Capt. Fauchey, Royal Gloster Militia
Rev. J. Furneaux, M. A. Plymouth
Capt. Farmar, Marines
Fountain Book Club, Huntingdon
Captain Flight, Marines
Charles Fuller, Esq.
Mrs. Fryar, Queen's Square

G.

Her Grace the Dutchess of Gordon
Right Honourable Lord Grey
The Honourable John Grey
The Honourable Mrs. John Grey
Sir Henry Goodricke, Bart.
Mrs. Gifford, Nerquis
Miss Gifford
Captain Gibbons, Marines
Lieutenant P. L. Gordon, Ditto
Lieutenant Errol Gordon, Ditto
Joseph Greaves, Esq. Liverpool
Mr. Green, Ditto
Mr. Thomas Gleaves, Ditto
William Godley, Esq. Chester
Rev. H. D. Griffith, Ditto
Mr. J. A. Gouldsbury, Ditto
George Grote, Esq. Westminster
Lieut. J. H. Griffith, Royal Navy

William Gillies, Esq. Crutched Friars
George Gordon, Esq. Parliament-str.
J. Gray, Esq. Lancaster-court, Strand
Rev. J. Gooch, D. D. Prebendary of Ely
Mark Grigg, Esq. Plymouth Dock
Mr. Glencross, Ditto
R. E. Gregory, Esq. Langar, Nottingham
R. Griffith, Esq. Caerhaen, Carnarvon
Mr. Gleed, Trinity Coll. Cambridge

H

Right Hon. the Marquis of Huntley
The Hon. Mr. Hill, Jesus Coll. Cambridge
Lieut. General John Hale
Humph. Hall, Esq. Manedon, Devon
The Honourable Mrs. Hall
J. Cawley Humberstone, Esq. Geversilt Park
John Haygarth, Esq. M. D. Chester
Mrs. Haygarth, Chester
Charles Henchman, Esq. Ditto
Charles Hamilton, Esq. Ditto
Henry Hesketh, Esq. Ditto
Robert Hodgson, Esq. Ditto
Mr. Hamilton, Ditto
William Houghton, Esq. M. D. Ditto
Major Hughes, Roy. Flintshire Militia
Richard Hale, Esq.
John Hale, Esq.
William Hodge, Esq. Bennet-street, Blackfriars
John Holman, Esq.
John Hunter, Esq.
Robert Hesketh, Esq. Gwoych, Denbighshire
Lieut. Higginson, Marines

Lieut. Hunt, Ditto
George Hayes, Esq. Plymouth
Mr. Haydon, Bookseller to His R. H. the Duke of Clarence, Plymouth, (twelve copies)
Mr. Hibbert, King's Coll. Cambridge
Mr. Hoxland, Plymouth Dock
A. Heywood, Esq. Liverpool
Mr. William Hillary, Ditto
Mr. William Heathcote, Ditto
Mr. Martin Hammill, Ditto
Mr. William Hadkinson, Ditto
Mr. Thomas Hornby, Ditto
John Howard, Esq. Ditto
Henry Hicks, Esq. Eastington, Gloucestershire
Captain Hicks, 32d Regiment
Edward Hill, Esq. Stonehouse, Gloucestershire
Mr. Hill, Dursley, Ditto
John Heriot, Esq. London
Reginald Heber, Esq. Malpas
Lieut. Col. Hay, Leith Hall
C. Huffum, Esq. Limehouse
Rev. T. Hunter, Waverham, Cheshire
Capt. A. Hawkins, N. Devon Militia
Rev. R. Hill, M. A. Hough, Cheshire
Rev. W. R. Humphreys, Carnarvon
—— Hussey, Esq.
—— Hussey, Esq.
Mr. Hornby, Trinity Coll. Cambridge
Rev. Mr. Hunter, Christ Coll. Ditto

J.

John Jackson, Esq. Huntingdon
Edward Jenner, Esq. M. D. Berkeley
W. Adair Jackson, Esq. Westminster
Col. Innes, Marines
Rev. R. Jackson, A. M. Babington.

Rev. R. P. Johnson, A. M. Ashton, Cheshire
Mr. Johnson, Congleton
John Jones, Esq. Rhagat, Denbigh
Mr. S. Jenner, Stroudwater
Mr. W. Jones, Emanuel Coll. Camb.

K.

Right Hon. Lord Kilmorey
Rev. J. Kentish, Plymouth
Lieutenant Kempster, Marines
Lieutenant Keates, Ditto
Lieutenant Katon, Ditto
John Kendal, Esq. Liverpool
Mr. John Kean, Ditto

L.

The Right Rev. Father in God, Beilby Lord Bishop of London
Lady Lloyd, Seymour-street
Honourable William Leslie
Mr. Lane, Trinity Coll. Cambridge
Hugh Leycester, Esq. Toft, Cheshire
G. Leycester, Esq. Ditto, (four copies)
Mrs. Leycester, (two copies)
Rev. O. Leycester, Knutsford, (2 do)
Charles Leycester, Esq. Charlton
H. L. Leycester, Esq. Royal Cheshire Militia
Mrs. Lane, Chester
Stephen Leeke, Esq. Ditto
Henry Lidgbud, Esq. London
Reverend Archdeacon Leigh, Lymm, Cheshire
Mrs. Leigh
Rev. N. C. Lane, Christ Coll. Camb-
Major Lindsay, Marines
Captain Lewis, Ditto

Mrs. Lloyd, Swan Hill, Shropshire
Wm. Henry Legrand, Esq. Devon
Mr. Law, London
Beeston Long, Esq. Ditto
Charles Long, Esq. Ditto
Thomas Ludbey, Esq. Ditto
Mr. Leyland, Liverpool
Rev. Mr. Lyne, Liskeard
Mr. Luscombe
Daniel Little, Esq. Plymouth
Joseph Lugger, Esq. Clerk of the Survey, Plymouth
William Lawrence, Esq. Plymouth
J. G. Lewis, Esq. Royal Cheshire Militia
J. R. Lloyd, Esq. Aston
John Legh, Esq. Bedford-square
Rev. James Lyon, A. M. Beestwick, Lancashire
Edm. Lyon, Esq. Newton, Cheshire
Mr. Liddle, Bodmin
Mrs. Lally, Catscluff, Cheshire

M.

Right Hon. Lord Henry Murray
Sir R. Mostyn, Bart. M.P. (2 copies)
Sir William Molesworth, Bart.
Lady Molesworth
Captain Madden, Marines
Captain Munro, Ditto
Captain Miller, Ditto
Lieutenant Martin, Ditto
Lieutenant H. Monteith, Ditto
Rob. Mowbray Esq. M. D. Plymouth
Vaughan May, Esq. Ditto
Lieut. M'Kenzie, Royal Fuzileers
Thomas Marsden, Esq. Chester
Rev. T. Maddock, A· M. Ditto

Thomas Moulson, Esq. Ditto
Mr. Midgely, Liverpool
Mr. G. Metcalf, Ditto
Rev. William Metcalf, A. M. Ely
Mr. Murril, Ditto
Mr. William Mathews, Liverpool
Mr. Mitchel, Ovendon, near Halifax
Mr· John Mills, London
— Martin, Esq. Crown-court, West-
    minster
Alexander Milne, Esq. Aberdeen
Mayow Mayow, Esq. Ely Place
L. R. Mackintosh Esq. London
Mr. Morril, St. John's Coll. Camb.

N.

Sir Stafford Henry Northcote, Bart.
Captain Nicholson, Marines
Rev. William Nelson, Chester
William Nichols, Esq. Ditto
Mr. Robert Norris, Liverpool
Mr. W. Neilson, Ditto, (2 copies)
Thomas Netherton, Esq. Plymouth

O.

Paul Orchard, Esq. M. P.
Captain Ollney, Royal Glos. Militia
Mr. Okell, Chester

P.

Rt. Hon. Lord Penryhn (two copies)
Lady Penryhn (two copies)
Mrs. Puleston, Wrexham
Mrs. Puleston, Gwyranney, two copies
Rev. P. Puleston, Rhuabon
Col. Percival, Marines
Thomas Pennant, Esq. F. R. S.
George Beeston Prescot, Esq. West-
    minster

G. W. Prescot, Esq. Theobalds, Herts
Peter Patten, Esq. Chester
Charles Potts, Esq. Ditto
Frederick Phillips, Esq. Ditto
Mr. Parry, Ditto
Mrs. Martha Price, Ditto
Mrs. Parry Price, Ditto
Monsieur Parisot de St. Marie, Ditto
Lt. Pownoll, Marines
Charles Pasheller, Esq. Huntingdon
John Peachey, Esq.
Ralph Peters, Esq.- Liverpool
Mr. Robert Preston, Ditto
Rev. Charles Prescot, Stockport
W. Pownoll, Esq. Chorlton, Cheshire
Rev. T. Porter, Plymouth
Robert Podmore, Esq. Hackney
Capt. Pearce, Marines
Mr. Purchase, Cambridge
Domville Poole, Esq. Lymm
Rev. J. Porter, D. D. Smarden, Kent
Thomas Parker, Esq. Royal Cheshire
    Militia
Mrs. C. Pennant, Upper Grosv. str.

R.

Lady Ramsden, Byrom, Yorkshire
Bagot Read, Esq. Chester
Edward Read, Esq. Ditto
John Ready, Esq. Ditto
Mr. Rowlands, Ditto
Mrs. Rodd, Plymouth
R. Rosdew, Ditto
Robert Richmond, Esq. Liverpool
Wm. Rig, Esq. Ditto
Mr. Wm. Rigby, Ditto
Mr. Wm. Read, Ditto
Captain Ross, 25th Regiment
David Ricardo, Esq. Stock Exchange

Rich. Richardson, Esq. Capenhurst Cheshire

W. Richardson, Esq. Royal Cheshire Militia

Edw. Ravenscroft, Esq. Harley-street, Cavendish-square

Miss Ravenscroft, Middlewich

Thomas Rutt, Esq. Homerton

John Russel, Esq. Westminster

S.

Right Hon. the Marq. of Salisbury

Right Hon. the Earl of Stamford

Right Hon. Lord Stanley, Tr. College, Cambridge

Sir J. S. M. Stanley, Bart.

Col. Souter, Marines

Col. Sandys, Ditto

Col. Spry, Ditto

Captain Skinner, Ditto

Lieut. Short, Ditto

Robert Sargent, Esq. Plymouth

Græme Spence, Esq. Ditto

—— Senior, Esq. Ditto

James St. Aubyn, Esq. Ditto

John Stapleton, Esq. Ditto

Captain Smith, Marines

Joseph Snow, Esq. Chester

Mr. S. Seller, Ditto

Mr. W. Seller, Ditto

Mr. Smith, Ditto

Mr. J. Smith, Emanuel Coll. Cambr.

Mr. W. Skelhorne, Liverpool

Mr. J. Stanton, Ditto

David Shuckforth, Esq. Royal Navy

Mr. G. Shelford, Trinity Hall, Camb.

Mrs. Seete

Mrs. Seel, Bloomsbury-square

Capt. Symonds, R. Gloucester Militia

Mr. Symonds, Oxford University

Edward Sheppard, Esq. Islington

Social Library, Stroud

Rev. James Saunders, A. M. Ely

C. T. Shackerley, Esq. R. Ches. Mil.

Rev. J. Smith, D. D. Master of Caius College, Cambridge

Mr. Stephens, Cambridge

Rev. Mr. Stephens, Fell. of St. John's College, Ditto

John Sill, Esq. R. Chester Militia, (2)

Henry Sweeting, Esq. Huntingdon

James Standerwick, Esq. Islington

Mr. Sidebotham, Wynnstay

Roger Swettenham, Esq. Summerford Booths

—— Swain, Esq.

T.

Mrs. Tarleton, Liverpool

Mrs. Ann Tarleton, Ditto, (2 copies)

T. Tarleton, Esq. Boldsworth Castle, (two copies)

John Tarleton, Esq. M. P. Liverpool (two copies)

Clay. Tarleton, Esq. Ditto, (2 copies)

Mrs. Turner, Wrexham

Colonel Tupper, Marines

Edward Townshend, Esq. Chester

Thomas Townshend, Esq. Ditto

G. S. Townshend, Esq. Ditto

William Thomas, Esq. Ditto

Mascie Taylor, Esq. Ditto

Mrs. S. Townshend, Ditto

Sam. Tolfrey, Esq. London, (2 copies)

Thomas Taylor, Esq. Lymm, Cheshire

Ed. Thornycroft, Esq. Thornycroft, Cheshire

Rev. G. Travis, Archdeac. of Chester

Rev. E. Thelwall, Llanbeder, Denbighshire

T. Trafford, Esq. R. Chester Militia

William Tatnal, Esq. Westminster

Edward Thornton, Esq. Stroudwater

G. Teait, Esq. Naval Storekeeper, Plymouth

Mr. Trueman, Plymouth, (two copies)

S. Tolfrey, Esq. Bickham, near Exeter

U.

Mr. William Unsworth, Liverpool

V.

Sir R. W. Vaughan, M. P. Bart.

Griffith Howel Vaughan, Esq. Rhug, Merioneth.

S. Vernon, Esq. Middlewich

R. H. Vivian, Esq. Plymouth

Rev. G. Vanbrugh, Haughton, Lancashire

W.

Lady Williams Wynn

Watkin Williams, Esq. M. P.

Mrs. Ward, Chester

Rev. Peploe Ward, A. M. Prebendary of Ely

Mrs. Peploe Ward

Rev. T. Ward, A. M. Prebendary of Chester

Mrs. Wettenhall, Chester

Mrs. Wilkinson, Ditto

Mrs. Witter, Ditto

Edw. Ommaney Wrench, Esq. Ditto

Mr. P. Wilkinson, Ditto

Samuel Wathen, Esq. New House, Gloucestershire

Nathaniel Wathen, Esq.

H. Wise, Esq. Brazen Nose College.

G. Wardle, Esq. Hart's Heath, Flintshire

Mrs. Wardle, Tower, Flintshire

Isaac Wood, Esq. Winsford, Cheshire

Mrs. Williams, Swan Hill, Shropshire

Mrs. Wynne, Plasnewydd, Denbighsh.

Mrs. Wynne, Chester-str. Wrexham

Mrs. Wynne, Hope-street, Ditto

Mr. Aaron Wills, Plymouth

Mr. Wilkinson, Ditto

John Webber, Esq.

Thomas Winsloe, Esq.

T. Par. Wilsfort, Throgmorton-str.

Colonel Wemyss, Marines

Cap. Whatley, R. Gloustershire Militia

C. Willoughby, Esq. Westminster

Mrs. Woodcock, Bath

T. Wilkinson, Esq. Chatham Place

St. And. Ward, Esq. Hooton Panell, Yorkshire

— Witmore, Esq. Apley, Shropshire

R. Wynne, Esq. Garthuen, Denbighsh.

N. E. Wynne, Esq. Llewessog, Ditto

Mr. R. Wright, Liverpool

Mr. T. Wood, Emanuel Coll. Cambr.

Y.

P. Yorke, Esq. Erthig, Denbighshire

Mrs. Yorke

Miss Young, Llanerch Park

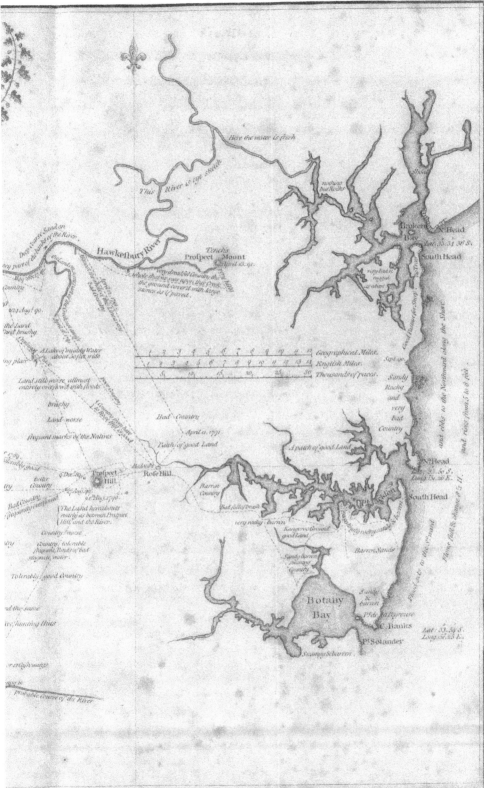

Here the river is fresh

This River is one stretch

nothing but Rocks

Shoals

Broken Bay
Latt. 33. 34. 30 S.

N: Head

South Head

Deep coarse Sand on the bottom of the River.

Very bad part of the bottom of the River.

May short off

Hawkesbury River

Tench's Prospect Mount
April 18. 91.

very dindled Country the hills the ground cover'd with large stones as if paved.

Country

very bad ragged rocks above

Coal Rams for Sheep

24 Aug: 90.

the Land Level brushy

ing place

A Lake of muddy Water about 30 feet wide

Sept: 90.

Sandy Rocky and very bad Country

Land still worse almost entirely overflow'd with floods

Geographical Miles.

English Miles.

Thousands of paces.

brushy

Land worse

frequent marks of the Natives

Bad Country

April 11. 1791

Patch of good Land

A patch of good Land

N: Head
Latt. 33. 50 S.
Long: 151. 26 E.

9 Dec: 90

better Country

Rose Hill

Prospect Hill

Midway

South Head

1739
tolerably good

Aug: 90

Bad Country frequently overflow'd

Barren Country

Bad falling brush

very rocky barren

Country house

The Land hereabouts mainly as between Prospect Hill and the River.

Kangaroo Ground good Land

Barren Sands

Country. tolerable frequent Ponds of bad sea water.

Sandy barren swampy Country

Tolerably good Country

Sandy & barren

Botany Bay

P:t de la Pérouse

C. Banks

and the same

ire hunting Huts

Steep, full & changes at 8 H.

and ebbs to the Northward along the Shore

and rises from 5 to 8 feet

Flood sets to the round

Latt: 33. 59 S.
Long: 151.25 E.

P:t Solander

Swampy & barren

or of Customers

Probable course of the River

J. Walker sculp.t

A COMPLETE ACCOUNT, &c.

CHAPTER I.

A Retrospect of the State of the Colony of PORT JACKSON, *on the Date of my former Narrative, in* July, 1788.

Pʀᴇᴠɪᴏᴜs to commencing any farther account of the subject, which I am about to treat, such a retrospection of the circumstances and situation of the settlement, at the conclusion of my former Narrative, as shall lay its state before the reader, seems necessary, in order to connect the present with the past.

The departure of the first fleet of ships for Europe, on the 14th of July, 1788, had been long impatiently expected; and had filled us with anxiety, to communicate to our friends an account of our situation; describing the progress of improvement, and the probability of success, or failure, in our enterprise. That men should judge very oppositely on so doubtful and precarious an event, will hardly surprise.

1788. Such relations could contain little besides the sanguineness of hope, and the enumeration of hardships and difficulties, which former accounts had not led us to expect. Since our disembarkation, in the preceding January, the efforts of every one had been unremittingly exerted, to deposite the public stores in a state of shelter and security, and to erect habitations for ourselves. We were eager to escape from tents, where a fold of canvas, only, interposed to check the vertic beams of the sun in summer, and the chilling blasts of the south in winter. A markee pitched, in our

B

finest season, on an English lawn; or a transient view of those gay camps, near the metropolis, which so many remember, naturally draws forth careless and unmeaning exclamations of rapture, which attach ideas of pleasure only, to this part of a soldier's life. But an encampment amidst the rocks and wilds of a new country, aggravated by the miseries of bad diet, and incessant toil, will find few admirers.

1788. Nor were our exertions less unsuccessful than they were laborious. Under wretched covers of thatch lay our provisions and stores, exposed to destruction from every flash of lightning, and every spark of fire. A few of the convicts had got into huts; but almost all the officers, and the whole of the soldiery, were still in tents.

In such a situation, where knowledge of the mechanic arts afforded the surest recommendation to notice, it may be easily conceived, that attention to the parade duty of the troops, gradually diminished. Now were to be seen officers and soldiers not " trailing the puissant pike," but felling the ponderous gum-tree, or breaking the stubborn clod. And though " the broad falchion did not in a ploughshare end," the possession of a spade, a wheelbarrow, or a dunghill, was more coveted than the most refulgent arms in which heroism ever dazzled. Those hours, which in other countries are devoted to martial acquirements, were here consumed in the labours of the sawpit, the forge, and the quarry.*

Of the two ships of war, the Sirius and Supply, the latter was incessantly employed in transporting troops, convicts, and stores,

---

* " The Swedish prisoners, taken at the battle of Pultowa, were transported by the Czar Peter to the most remote parts of Siberia, with a view to civilize the natives of the country, and teach them the arts the Swedes possessed. In this hopeless situation, all traces of discipline and subordination, between the different ranks, were quickly obliterated. The soldiers, who were husbandmen and artificers, found out their superiority, and assumed it: the officers became their servants." VOLTAIRE.

to Norfolk Island; and the Sirius in preparing for a voyage to some port, where provisions for our use might be purchased, the expected supply from England not having arrived. It is but justice to the officers and men of both these ships to add, that, on all occasions, they fully shared every hardship and fatigue with those on shore.

1788. On the convicts the burden fell yet heavier: necessity compelled us to allot to them the most slavish and laborious employments. Those operations, which in other countries are performed by the brute creation, were here effected by the exertions of men: but this ought not to be considered a grievance; because they had always been taught to expect it, as the inevitable consequence of their offences against society. Severity was rarely exercised on them; and justice was administered without partiality or discrimination. Their ration of provisions, except in being debarred from an allowance of spirits, was equal to that which the marines received. Under these circumstances I record with pleasure, that they behaved better than had been predicted of them—To have expected sudden and complete reformation of conduct, were romantic and chimerical.

Our cultivation of the land was yet in its infancy. We had hitherto tried only the country contiguous to Sydney. Here the governor had established a government-farm; at the head of which a competent person of his own household was placed, with convicts to work under him. Almost the whole of the officers likewise accepted of small tracts of ground, for the purpose of raising grain and vegetables: but experience proved to us, that the soil would produce neither without manure; and as this was not to be procured, our vigour soon slackened; and most of the farms (among which was the one belonging to government) were successively abandoned.

1788. With the natives we were very little more acquainted than on our arrival in the country. Our intercourse with them was neither frequent or cordial. They seemed studiously to avoid us, either from fear, jealousy, or hatred. When they met with unarmed stragglers, they sometimes killed, and sometimes wounded them. I confess that, in common with many others, I was inclined to attribute this conduct, to a spirit of malignant levity. But a farther acquaintance with them, founded on several instances of their humanity and generosity, which shall be noticed in their proper places, has entirely reversed my opinion; and led me to conclude, that the unprovoked outrages committed upon them, by unprincipled individuals among us, caused the evils we had experienced. To prevent them from being plundered of their fishing-tackle and weapons of war, a proclamation was issued, forbidding their sale among us; but it was not attended with the good effect which was hoped for from it.

During this period, notwithstanding the want of fresh provisions and vegetables, and almost constant exposure to the vicissitudes of a variable climate, disease rarely attacked us; and the number of deaths, was too inconsiderable to deserve mention.

Norfolk Island had been taken possession of, by a party detached for that purpose, early after our arrival. Few accounts of it had yet reached us. And here I beg leave to observe, that as I can speak of this island only from the relations of others, never having myself been there, I shall in every part of this work mention it as sparingly as possible. And this more especially, as it seems probable, that some of those gentlemen, who from accurate knowledge, and long residence on it, are qualified to write its history, will oblige the world with such a publication.

CHAPTER II.

Transactions of the Colony from the sailing of the first Fleet in July, 1788, to the Close of that Year.

It was impossible to behold without emotion the departure of the ships. On their speedy arrival in England perhaps hinged our fate; by hastening our supplies to us.

On the 20th of July, the Supply sailed for Norfolk Island, and returned to us on the 26th of August; bringing no material news, except that the soil was found to suit grain, and other seeds, which had been sown in it, and that a species of flax-plant was discovered to grow spontaneously on the island.

1788. A survey of the harbour of Port Jackson was now undertaken, in order to compute the number of canoes, and inhabitants, which it might contain: sixty-seven canoes, and 147 people were counted. No estimate. however, of even tolerable accuracy, can be drawn from so imperfect a datum; though it was perhaps the best in our power to acquire.

In July and August, we experienced more inclement tempestuous weather than had been observed at any former period of equal duration. And yet it deserves to be remarked, in honour of the climate, that, although our number of people exceeded 900, not a single death happened in the latter month.

The dread of want in a country destitute of natural resource is ever peculiarly terrible. We had long turned our eyes with impatience towards the sea, cheered by the hope of seeing supplies from England approach. But none arriving, on the 2d of October the Sirius sailed for the Cape of Good Hope, with directions to purchase provisions there, for the use of our garrison.

A new settlement, named by the governor Rose Hill, 16 miles inland, was established on the 3d of November, the soil here being judged better than that around Sydney. A small redoubt was thrown up, and a captain's detachment posted in it, to protect the convicts who were employed to cultivate the ground.

The two last of the transports left us for England on the 19th of November, intending to make their passage by Cape Horn. There now remained with us only the Supply. Sequestered and cut off as we were from the rest of civilized nature, their absence carried the effect of desolation.

About this time a convict, of the name of Daly, was hanged, for a burglary: this culprit, who was a notorious thief and impostor, was the author of a discovery of a gold mine, a few months before: a composition resembling ore mingled with earth, which he pretended to have brought from it, he produced. After a number of attendant circumstances, too ludicrous and contemptible to relate, which befel a party, who were sent under his guidance to explore this second Peru, he at last confessed, that he had broken up an old pair of buckles, and mixed the pieces with sand and stone; and on essaying the composition, the brass was detected. The fate of this fellow I should not deem worth recording, did it not lead to the following observation:—that the utmost circumspection is necessary to prevent imposition, in those who give accounts of what they see in unknown countries. We found the convicts particularly happy in fertility of invention, and exaggerated descriptions. Hence large fresh water rivers, valuable ores, and quarries of limestone, chalk, and marble, were daily proclaimed soon after we had landed. At first we hearkened with avidity to such accounts; but perpetual disappointments taught us to listen with caution, and to believe from demonstration only.

Unabated animosity continued to prevail between the natives and us : in addition to former losses, a soldier and several convicts suddenly disappeared, and were never afterwards heard of. Three convicts were also wounded, and one killed by them, near Botany Bay: similar to the vindictive spirit which Mr. Cook found to exist among their countrymen at Endeavour river, they more than once attempted to set fire to combustible matter, in order to annoy us. Early on the morning of the 18th of December, word was brought that they were assembled in force, near the brick-kilns, which stand but a mile from the town of Sydney. The terror of those who brought the first intelligence magnified the number to two thousand ; a second messenger diminished it to four hundred. A detachment, under the command of an officer was ordered to march immediately, and reconnoitre them. The officer soon returned, and reported, that about fifty Indians had appeared at the brick-kilns ; but upon the convicts, who were at work there, pointing their spades and shovels at them, in the manner of guns, they had fled into the woods.

Tired of this state of petty warfare and endless uncertainty, the governor at length determined to adopt a decisive measure, by capturing some of them, and retaining them by force ; which we supposed would either inflame the rest to signal vengeance, in which case we should know the worst, and provide accordingly: or else it would induce an intercourse, by the report which our prisoners would make of the mildness and indulgence with which we used them. And farther, it promised to unveil the cause of their mysterious conduct, by putting us in possession of their reasons for harassing and destroying our people, in the manner I have related. Boats were accordingly ordered to be got ready, and every preparation made, which could lead to the attainment of our object.

But as this subject deserves to be particularly detailed, I shall, notwithstanding its being just within the period of time which this chapter professes to comprise, allot it a separate place, in the beginning of the next.

Nor can I close this part of my work without congratulating both the reader and the author. New matter now presents itself. A considerable part of the foregoing chapters had been related before, either by others or myself. I was however, unavoidably compelled to insert it, in order to preserve unbroken that chain of detail, and perspicuity of arrangement, at which books professing to convey information should especially aim.

CHAPTER III.

Transactions of the Colony, from the Commencement of the Year 1789, *until the End of March.*

Pursuant to his resolution, the governor on the 31st of December sent two boats, under the command of Lieutenant Ball of the Supply, and Lieutenant George Johnston of the marines, down the harbour, with directions to those officers to seize and carry off some of the natives. The boats proceeded to Manly Cove, where several Indians were seen standing on the beach, who were enticed by courteous behaviour and a few presents to enter into conversation. A proper opportunity being presented, our people rushed in among them, and seized two men: the rest fled; but the cries of the captives soon brought them back, with many others, to their rescue: and so desperate were their struggles, that, in spite of every effort on our side, only one of them was secured; the other effected his escape. The boats put off without delay; and an attack from the shore instantly commenced: they threw spears, stones, firebrands, and whatever else presented itself, at the boats; nor did they retreat, agreeable to their former custom, until many musquets were fired over them.

The prisoner was now fastened by ropes to the thwarts of the boat; and when he saw himself irretrievably disparted from his countrymen, set up the most piercing and lamentable cries of distress. His grief, however, soon diminished: he accepted and eat of some broiled fish which was given to him, and sullenly submitted to his destiny.

C

1789. When the news of his arrival at Sydney was announced, I went with every other person to see him: he appeared to be about thirty years old, not tall, but robustly made; and of a countenance which, under happier circumstances, I thought would display manliness and sensibility; his agitation was excessive, and the clamourous crowds who flocked around him did not contribute to lessen it. Curiosity and observation seemed, nevertheless, not to have wholly deserted him; he shewed the effect of novelty upon ignorance; he wondered at all he saw: though broken and interrupted with dismay, his voice was soft and musical, when its natural tone could be heard; and he readily pronounced with tolerable accuracy the names of things which were taught him. To our ladies he quickly became extraordinarily courteous, a sure sign that his terror was wearing off.

Every blandishment was used to soothe him, and it had its effect. As he was entering the governor's house, some one touched a small bell which hung over the door: he started with horror and astonishment; but in a moment after was reconciled to the noise, and laughed at the cause of his perturbation. When pictures were shewn to him, he knew directly those which represented the human figure: among others, a very large handsome print of her royal highness the Dutchess of Cumberland being produced, he called out, woman, a name by which we had just before taught him to call the female convicts. Plates of birds and beasts were also laid before him; and many people were led to believe, that such as he spoke about and pointed to were known to him. But this must have been an erroneous conjecture, for the elephant, rhinoceros, and several others, which we must have discovered did they exist in the country, were of the number. Again, on the other hand, those he did not point out, were equally unknown to him.

1789. His curiosity here being satiated, we took him to a large

brick house, which was building for the governor's residence: being about to enter, he cast up his eyes, and seeing some people lean-
ing out of a window on the first story, he exclaimed aloud, and testified the most extravagant surprise. Nothing here was observed
to fix his attention so strongly as some tame fowls, who were feeding near him: our dogs also he particularly noticed; but seemed
more fearful than fond of them.

He dined at a side-table at the governor's; and eat heartily of
fish and ducks, which he first cooled. Bread and salt meat he
smelled at, but would not taste: all our liquors he treated in the
same manner, and could drink nothing but water. On being
shewn that he was not to wipe his hands on the chair which he
sat upon, he used a towel which was gave to him, with great
cleanliness and decency.

In the afternoon his hair was closely cut, his head combed, and
his beard shaved; but he would not submit to these operations until he had seen them performed on another person, when he readily acquiesced. His hair, as might be supposed, was filled with
vermin, whose destruction seemed to afford him great triumph;
nay, either revenge, or pleasure, prompted him to eat them!
but on our expressing disgust and abhorrence he left it off.

To this succeeded his immersion in a tub of water and soap,
where he was completely washed and scrubbed from head to foot;
after which a shirt, a jacket, and a pair of trowsers, were put
upon him. Some part of this ablution I had the honour to perform, in order that I might ascertain the real colour of the skin
of these people. My observation then was (and it has since been
confirmed in a thousand other instances) that they are as black
as the lighter cast of the African negroes.

Many unsuccessful attempts were made to learn his name; the
governor therefore called him Manly, from the cove in which he

was captured: this cove had received its name from the manly undaunted behaviour of a party of natives seen there, on our taking possession of the country.

To prevent his escape, a handcuff with a rope attached to it, was fastened around his left wrist, which at first highly delighted him; he called it ' *Ben-gàd-ee* ' (or ornament), but his delight changed to rage and hatred when he discovered its use. His supper he cooked himself: some fish were given to him for this purpose, which, without any previous preparation whatever, he threw carelessly on the fire, and when they became warm took them up, and first rubbed off the scales, peeled the outside with his teeth, and eat it; afterwards he gutted them, and laying them again on the fire, completed the dressing, and eat them.

A convict was selected to sleep with him, and to attend him wherever he might go. When he went with his keeper into his apartment he appeared very restless and uneasy while a light was kept in; but on its extinction, he immediately lay down and composed himself.

Sullenness and dejection trongly marked his countenance on the following morning; to amuse him, he was taken around the camp, and to the observatory: casting his eyes to the opposite shore from the point where he stood, and seeing the smoke of fire lighted by his countrymen, he looked earnestly at it, and sighing deeply two or three times, ttered the word ' *gweè-un* ' (fire).

His loss of spirits had not, however, the effect of impairing his appetite; eight fish, each weighing about a pound, constituted his breakfast, which he dressed as before. When he had finished his repast, he turned his back to the fire in a musing posture, and crept so close to it, that his shirt was caught by the flame; luckily his keeper soon extinguished it; but he was so terrified at the accident, that he was with difficulty persuaded to put on a second.

1st. January, 1789. To-day being new-year's-day, most of the officers were invited to the governor's table: Manly dined heartily on fish and roasted pork; he was seated on a chest near a window, out of which, when he had done eating, he would have thrown his plate, had he not been prevented: during dinner-time a band of music played in an adjoining apartment; and after the cloth was removed, one of the company sang in a very soft and superior style; but the powers of melody were lost on Manly, which disappointed our expectations, as he had before shown pleasure and readiness in imitating our tunes. Stretched out on his chest, and putting his hat under his head, he fell asleep.

To convince his countrymen that he had received no injury from us, the governor took him in a boat down the harbour, that they might see and converse with him: when the boat arrived, and lay at a little distance from the beach, several Indians who had retired at her approach, on seeing Manly, returned: he was greatly affected, and shed tears. At length they began to converse. Our ignorance of the language prevented us from knowing much of what passed; it was, however, easily understood that his friends asked him why he did not jump overboard, and rejoin them. He only sighed, and pointed to the fetter on his leg, by which he was bound.

In going down the harbour he had described the names by which they distinguish its numerous creeks and headlands: he was now often heard to repeat that of *Wee-rong* (Sydney), which was doubtless to inform his countrymen of the place of his captivity; and perhaps to invite them to rescue him. By this time his gloom was chaced away, and he parted from his friends without testifying reluctance. His vivacity and good humour continued all the evening, and produced so good an effect on his appetite, that he eat for supper two Kanguroo rats, each of the size of a moderate rabbit, and in addition not less than three pounds of fish.

Two days after he was taken on a similar excursion; but to our surprise the natives kept aloof, and would neither approach the shore, or discourse with their countryman: we could get no explanation of this difficulty, which seemed to affect us more than it did him. Uncourteous as they were, he performed to them an act of attentive benevolence; seeing a basket made of bark, used by them to carry water, he conveyed into it two hawks and another bird, which the people in the boat had shot, and carefully covering them over, left them as a present to his old friends. But indeed the gentleness and humanity of his disposition frequently displayed themselves: when our children, stimulated by wanton curiosity, used to flock around him, he never failed to fondle them, and, if he were eating at the time, constantly offered them the choicest part of his fare.

February, 1789. His reserve, from want of confidence in us, continued gradually to wear away: he told us his name, and Manly gave place to Ar-ab-a-noo. Bread he began to relish; and tea he drank with avidity: strong liquors he would never taste, turning from them with disgust and abhorrence. Our dogs and cats had ceased to be objects of fear, and were become his greatest pets, and constant companions at table. One of our chief amusements, after the cloth was removed, was to make him repeat the names of things in his language, which he never hesitated to do with the utmost alacrity, correcting our pronunciation when erroneous. Much information relating to the customs and manners of his country was also gained from him: but as this subject will be separately and amply treated, I shall not anticipate myself by partially touching on it here.

On the 2d of February died Captain John Shea of the marines, after a lingering illness: he was interred on the following day, with the customary military honours, amidst the regret of all who knew him. In consequence of his decease, appointments for the promotion of the oldest officer of each subordinate rank were signed by the major commandant of the marine battalion, until the pleasure of the lords of the admiralty should be notified *.

On the 17th of February the Supply again sailed for Norfolk Island. The governor went down the harbour in her, and carried Arabanoo with him, who was observed to go on board with distrust and reluctance; when he found she was under sail, every effort was tried without success to exhilarate him; at length, an opportunity being presented, he plunged overboard, and struck out for the nearest shore: believing that those who were left behind would fire at him, he attempted to dive, at which he was known to be very expert: but this was attended with a difficulty which he had not foreseen: his clothes proved so buoyant, that he was unable to get more than his head under water: a boat was immediately dispatched after him, and picked him up, though not without struggles and resistance on his side. When brought on board, he appeared neither afraid or ashamed of what he had done, but sat apart, melancholy and dispirited, and continued so until he saw the governor and his other friends descend into a boat, and heard himself called upon to accompany them: he sprang forward, and his cheerfulness and alacrity of temper immediately returned, and lasted during the remainder of the day. The dread of being carried away, on an element of whose boundary he could form no conception, joined to the uncertainty of our intention towards him, unquestionably caused him to act as he did.

* These appointments were confirmed by the admiralty.

One of the prinicipal effects which we had supposed the seizure and captivity of Arabanoo would produce, seemed yet at as great a distance as ever; the natives neither manifested signs of increased hostility on his account, or attempted to ask any explanation of our conduct through the medium of their countrymen who was in our possession, and who they knew was treated with no farther harshness than in being detained among us. Their forbearance of open and determined attack upon us can be accounted for only by recollecting their knowledge of our numbers, and their dread of our fire-arms: that they wanted not sufficient provocation to do so, will appear from what I am about to relate.

March, 1789. Sixteen convicts left their work at the brick-kilns without leave, and marched to Botany Bay, with a design to attack the natives, and to plunder them of their fishing-tackle and spears: they had armed themselves with their working tools and large clubs. When they arrived near the bay, a body of Indians, who had probably seen them set out, and had penetrated their intention from experience, suddenly fell upon them. Our heroes were immediately routed, and separately endeavoured to effect their escape by any means which were left. In their flight one was killed, and seven were wounded, for the most part very severely: those who had the good fortune to outstrip their comrades and arrive in camp, first gave the alarm; and a detachment of marines, under an officer, was ordered to march to their relief. The officer arrived too late to repel the Indians; but he brought in the body of the man that was killed, and put an end to the pursuit. The governor was justly incensed at what had happened, and instituted the most rigorous scrutiny into the cause which had produced it. At first the convicts were unanimous in affirming, that they were quietly picking *sweet-tea,* * when they were without provocation assaulted by the natives, with whom they had no wish to quarrel. Some of them, however, more irresolute than the rest, at last disclosed the purpose for which the expedition had been undertaken ; and the whole were ordered to be severely flogged : Arabanoo was present at the infliction of the punishment ; and was made to comprehend the cause and the necessity of it ; but he displayed on the occasion symptoms of disgust and terror only.

March, 1789. On the 24th instant the Supply arrived from Norfolk Island, and Lord Howe Island, bringing from the latter place three turtles.

An awful and terrible example of justice took place towards the close of this month, which I record with regret, but which it would be disingenuous to suppress.—Six marines, the flower of our battalion, were hanged by the public executioner, on the sentence of a criminal court, composed entirely of their own officers, for having at various times robbed the public stores of flour, meat, spirits, tobacco, and many other articles.

---

* A vegetable creeper found growing on the rocks, which yields, on infusion in hot water, a sweet astringent taste, whence it derives its name : to its virtues the healthy state of the soldiery and convicts may be greatly attributed. It was drank universally.

CHAPTER IV.

Transactions of the Colony in April and May, 1789.

A<small>N</small> extraordinary calamity was now observed among the natives. Repeated accounts brought by our boats of finding bodies of the Indians in all the coves and inlets of the harbour, caused the gentlemen of our hospital to procure some of them for the purposes of examination and anatomy. On inspection, it appeared that all the parties had died a natural death: pustules, similar to those occasioned by the small pox, were thickly spread on the bodies; but how a disease, to which our former observations had led us to suppose them strangers, could at once have introduced itself, and have spread so widely, seemed inexplicable.* Whatever might be the cause, the existence of the malady could no longer be doubted. Intelligence was brought that an Indian family lay sick in a neighbouring cove: the governor, attended by Arabanoo, and a surgeon, went in a boat immediately to the spot. Here they found an old man stretched before a few lighted sticks, and a boy of nine

---

* No solution of this difficulty had been given when I left the country, in December, 1791. I can, therefore, only propose queries for the ingenuity of others to exercise itself upon: Is it a disease indigenous to the country? Did the French ships under Monsieur de Peyrouse introduce it? let it be remembered that they had now been departed more than a year; and we had never heard of its existence on board of them.—Had it travelled across the continent from its western shore, where Dampier and other European voyagers had formerly landed?— Was it introduced by Mr. Cook?—Did we give it birth here? No person among us had been afflicted with the disorder since we had quitted the Cape of Good Hope, seventeen months before. It is true, that our surgeons had brought out variolous matter in bottles; but to infer that it was produced from this cause were a supposition so wild as to be unworthy of consideration.

or ten years old pouring water on his head, from a shell which he held in his hand: near them lay a female child dead, and a little farther off, its unfortunate mother: the body of the woman shewed that famine, superadded to disease, had occasioned her death: eruptions covered the poor boy from head to foot; and the old man was so reduced, that he was with difficulty got into the boat. Their situation rendered them incapable of escape, and they quietly submitted to be led away. Arabanoo, contrary to his usual character, seemed at first unwilling to render them any assistance; but his shyness soon wore off, and he treated them with the kindest attention. Nor would he leave the place until he had buried the corpse of the child: that of the woman he did not see from its situation; and as his countrymen did not point it out, the governor ordered that it should not be shewn to him. He scooped a grave in the sand with his hands, of no peculiarity of shape, which he lined completely with grass, and put the body into it, covering it also with grass; and then he filled up the hole, and raised over it a small mound with the earth which had been removed. Here the ceremony ended, unaccompanied by any invocation to a superior being, or any attendant circumstance whence an inference of their religious opinions could be deduced.

April, 1789. An uninhabited house, near the hospital, was allotted for their reception, and a cradle prepared for each of them. By the encouragement of Arabanoo, who assured them of protection, and the soothing behaviour of our medical gentlemen, they became at once reconciled to us, and looked happy and grateful at the change of their situation. Sickness and hunger had, however, so much exhausted the old man, that little hope was entertained of his recovery. As he pointed frequently to his throat, at the instance of Arabanoo, he tried to wash it with a gargle which was given to him; but the obstructed, tender state of the part rendered it impracticable. *Bàdo, bàdo* (water), was his cry: when brought to him, he drank largely at intervals of it. He was equally importunate for fire, being seized with shivering fits; and one was kindled. Fish were produced, to tempt him to eat; but he turned away his head, with signs of loathing. Nān-bar-ee (the boy), on the contrary, no sooner saw them than he leaped from his cradle, and eagerly seizing them, began to cook them. A warm bath being prepared, they were immersed in it; and after being thoroughly cleansed, they had clean shirts put on them, and were again laid in bed.

The old man lived but a few hours. He bore the pangs of dissolution with patient composure; and though he was sensible to the last moment, expired almost without a groan. Nanbaree appeared quite unmoved at the event; and surveyed the corpse of his father without emotion, simply exclaiming, *bò-ee* (dead). This surprised us; as the tenderness and anxiety of the old man about the boy had been very moving. Although barely able to raise his head, while so much strength was left to him, he kept looking into his child's cradle; he patted him gently on the bosom; and, with dying eyes, seemed to recommend him to our humanity and protection. Nanbaree was adopted by Mr. White, surgeon-general of the settlement, and became henceforth one of his family.

April, 1789. Arabanoo had no sooner heard of the death of his countryman, than he hastened to inter him. I was present at the ceremony, in company with the governor, captain Ball, and two or three other persons. It differed, by the accounts of those who were present at the funeral of the girl, in no respect from what had passed there in the morning, except that the grave was dug by a convict. But I was informed, that when intelligence of the death reached Arabanoo, he expressed himself with doubt whether he should bury, or burn the body; and seemed solicitous to ascertain which ceremony would be most gratifying to the governor.

Indeed, Arabanoo's behaviour, during the whole of the transactions of this day, was so strongly marked by affection to his countryman, and by confidence in us, that the governor resolved to free him from all farther restraint, and at once to trust to his generosity, and the impression which our treatment of him might have made, for his future residence among us: the fetter was accordingly taken off his leg.

In the evening, captain Ball and I crossed the harbour, and buried the corpse of the woman before mentioned.

Distress continued to drive them in upon us. Two more natives, one of them a young man, and the other his sister, a girl of fourteen years old, were brought in by the governor's boat, in a most deplorable state of wretchedness from the small-pox. The sympathy and affection of Arabanoo, which had appeared languid in the instance of Nanbaree and his father, here manifested themselves immediately. We conjectured that a difference of the tribes to which they belonged might cause the preference; but nothing afterwards happened to strengthen or confirm such a supposition. The young man died at the end of three days: the girl recovered, and was received as an inmate, with great kindness, in the family of Mrs. Johnson, the clergyman's wife. Her name was Bòo-ron; but from our mistake of pronunciation she acquired that of Abar-oo, by which she was generally known, and by which she will always be called in this work. She shewed, at the death of her brother more feeling than Nanbaree had witnessed for the loss of his father. When she found him dying, she crept to his side, and lay by him until forced by the cold to retire. No exclamation, or other sign of grief, however, escaped her for what had happened.

May, 1789. At sunset, on the evening of the 2d instant, the arrival of the Sirius, Captain Hunter, from the Cape of Good Hope, was proclaimed, and diffused universal joy and congratulation. The day of famine was at least procrastinated by the supply of flour and salt provisions she brought us.

The Sirius had made her passage to the Cape of Good Hope, by the route of Cape Horn, in exactly thirteen weeks. Her highest latitude was 57° 10′ south, where the weather proved intolerably cold. Ice, in great quantity, was seen for many days ; and in the middle of December (which is correspondent to the middle of June, in our hemisphere), water froze in open casks upon deck, in the moderate latitude of 44° degrees.

They were very kindly treated by the Dutch governor, and amply supplied by the merchants at the Cape, where they remained seven weeks. Their passage back was effected by Van Dieman's Land, near which, and close under Tasman's Head, they were in the utmost peril of being wrecked.

In this long run, which had extended round the circle, they had always determined their longitude, to the greatest nicety, by distances taken between the sun and moon, or between the moon and a star. But it falls to the lot of very few ships to possess such indefatigable and accurate observers as Captain Hunter, and Mr. (now Captain) Bradley, the first lieutenant of the Sirius.

May, 1789. I feel assured, that I have no reader who will not join in regretting the premature loss of Arabanoo, who died of the small-pox on the 18th instant, after languishing in it six days. From some imperfect marks and indents on his face, we were inclined to believe that he had passed this dreaded disorder. Even when the first symptoms of sickness seized him, we continued willing to hope that they proceeded from a different cause. But at length the disease burst forth with irresistible fury   It were superfluous

to say, that nothing which medical skill and unremitting attention could perform, were left unexerted to mitigate his sufferings,
and prolong a life, which humanity and affectionate concern towards his sick compatriots, unfortunately shortened.

During his sickness he reposed entire confidence in us. Although a stranger to medicine, and nauseating the taste of it, he
swallowed with patient submission innumerable drugs,* which
the hope of relief induced us to administer to him. The governor,
who particularly regarded him,† caused him to be buried in his
own garden, and attended the funeral in person.

The character of Arabanoo, as far as we had developed it, was
distinguished by a portion of gravity and steadiness, which our
subsequent acquaintance with his countrymen by no means led us
to conclude a national characteristic. In that daring, enterprizing
frame of mind, which, when combined with genius, constitutes
the leader of a horde of savages, or the ruler of a people, boasting
the power of discrimination and the resistance of ambition, he was
certainly surpassed by some of his successors, who afterwards lived
among us. His countenance was thoughtful, but not animated:
his fidelity and gratitude, particularly to his friend the governor,

---

* Very different had been his conduct on a former occasion of a similar kind. Soon after he was brought among us he was seized with a diarrhœa, for which he could by no persuasion be induced to swallow any of our prescriptions. After many ineffectual trials to
deceive, or overcome him, it was at length determined to let him pursue his own course,
and to watch if he should apply for relief to any of the productions of the country. He
was in consequence observed to dig fern-root, and to chew it. Whether the disorder
had passed its crisis, or whether the fern-root effected a cure, I know not ; but it is certain
that he became speedily well.

† The regard was reciprocal. His excellency had been ill but a short time before, when
Arabanoo had testified the utmost solicitude for his ease and recovery. It is probable that
he acquired, on this occasion, just notions of the benefit to be derived from medical assistance. A doctor is, among them, a person of consequence. It is certain that he latterly
estimated our professional gentlemen very highly.

were constant and undeviating, and deserve to be recorded. Although of a gentle and placable temper, we early discovered that he was impatient of indignity, and allowed of no superiority on our part. He knew that he was in our power; but the independence of his mind never forsook him. If the slightest insult were offered to him, he would return it with interest. At retaliation of merriment he was often happy; and frequently turned the laugh against his antagonist. He did not want docility; but either from the difficulty of acquiring our language, from the unskilfulness of his teachers, or from some natural defect, his progress in learning it was not equal to what we had expected. For the last three or four weeks of his life, hardly any restraint was laid upon his inclinations: so that had he meditated escape, he might easily have effected it. He was, perhaps; the only native who was ever attached to us from choice; and who did not prefer a precarious subsistence among wilds and precipices, to the comforts of a civilized system.

By his death, the scheme which had invited his capture was utterly defeated. Of five natives who had been brought among us, three had perished from a cause which, though unavoidable, it was impossible to explain to a people, who would condescend to enter into no intercourse with us. The same suspicious dread of our approach, and the same scenes of vengeance acted on unfortunate stragglers, continued to prevail.

CHAPTER V.

Transactions of the Colony until the Close of the Year 1789.

THE anniversary of his majesty's birth-day was celebrated, as heretofore, at the government-house, with loyal festivity. In the evening, the play of the Recruiting Officer was performed by a party of convicts, and honoured by the presence of his excellency, and the officers of the garrison. That every opportunity of escape from the dreariness and dejection of our situation should be eagerly embraced, will not be wondered at. The exhilarating effect of a splendid theatre is well known: and I am not ashamed to confess, that the proper distribution of three or four yards of stained paper, and a dozen farthing candles stuck around the mud walls of a con-vict-hut, failed not to diffuse general complacency on the counte-nances of sixty persons, of various descriptions, who were assembled to applaud the representation. Some of the actors acquitted them-selves with great spirit, and received the praises of the audience: a prologue and an epilogue, written by one of the performers, were also spoken on the occasion; which, although not worth inserting here, contained some tolerable allusions to the situation of the parties, and the novelty of a stage-representation in New South Wales.

Broken Bay, which was supposed to be completely explored, be-came again an object of research. On the sixth instant, the gover-nor, accompanied by a large party in two boats, proceeded thither.

E

Here they again wandered over piles of mis-shapen desolation, contemplating scenes of wild solitude, whose unvarying appearance renders them incapable of affording either novelty or gratification. But when they had given over the hope of farther discovery, by pursuing the windings of an inlet, which, from its appearance, was supposed to be a short creek, they suddenly found themselves at the entrance of a fresh water river, up which they proceeded twenty miles, in a westerly direction; and would have farther prosecuted their research, had not a failure of provisions obliged them to return. This river they described to be of considerable breadth, and of great depth; but its banks had hitherto presented nothing better than a counterpart of the rocks and precipices which surround Broken Bay.

June, 1789. A second expedition, to ascertain its course, was undertaken by his excellency, who now penetrated (measuring by the bed of the river) between 60 and 70 miles, when the farther progress of the boats was stopped by a fall. The water in every part was found to be fresh and good. Of the adjoining country, the opinions of those who had inspected it (of which number I was not) were so various, that I shall decline to record them. Some saw a rich and beautiful country; and others were so unfortunate as to discover little else than large tracts of low land, covered with reeds, and rank with the inundations of the stream, by which they had been recently covered. All parties, however, agreed, that the rocky, impenetrable country, seen on the first excursion, had ended nearly about the place whence the boats had then turned back. Close to the fall stands a very beautiful hill, which our adventurers mounted, and enjoyed from it an extensive prospect. Potatoes, maize, and garden seeds of various kinds were put into the earth, by the governor's order, on different parts of Richmond-hill, which was announced to be its name. The latitude of Richmond-hill, as observed by captain Hunter, was settled at 33° 36 south.

Here also the river received the name of Hawkesbury, in honour of the noble lord who bears that title.

Natives were found on the banks in several parts, many of whom were labouring under the small-pox. They did not attempt to commit hostilities against the boats; but on the contrary shewed every sign of welcome and friendship to the strangers.

At this period, I was unluckily invested with the command of the outpost at Rose Hill, which prevented me from being in the list of discoverers of the Hawkesbury. Stimulated, however, by a desire of acquiring a further knowledge of the country, on the 26th instant, accompanied by Mr. Arndell, assistant surgeon of the settlement, Mr. Lowes, surgeon's mate of the Sirius, two marines, and a convict, I left the redoubt at day-break, pointing our march to a hill, distant five miles, in a westerly or inland direction, which commands a view of the great chain of mountains, called Carmar-then-hills, extending from north to south farther than the eye can reach. Here we paused, surveying " the wild abyss; pondering our voyage." Before us lay the trackless immeasurable desert, in awful silence. At length, after consultation, we determined to steer west and by north, by compass, the make of the land in that quarter indicating the existence of a river. We continued to march all day through a country untrodden before by an European foot. Save that a melancholy crow now and then flew croaking over head, or a kanguroo was seen to bound at a distance, the picture of solitude was complete and undisturbed. At four o'clock in the afternoon we halted near a small pond of water, where we took up our residence for the night, lighted a fire, and prepared to cook our supper :—that was, to broil over a couple of ramrods a few slices of salt pork, and a crow which we had shot. At daylight we renewed our peregrination; and in an hour after we found ourselves on the banks of a river, nearly as broad as the Thames at Putney, and apparently of great depth, the current running very slowly in a northerly direction. Vast flocks of wild ducks were swimming in the stream; but after being once fired at, they grew so shy that we could not get near them a second time. Nothing is more certain than that the sound of a gun had never before been heard within many miles of this spot.

We proceeded upwards, by a slow pace, through reeds, thickets, and a thousand other obstacles, which impeded our progress, over coarse sandy ground, which had been recently inundated, though full forty feet above the present level of the river. Traces of the natives appeared at every step, sometimes in their hunting-huts, which consist of nothing more than a large piece of bark, bent in the middle, and open at both ends, exactly resembling two cards, set up to form an acute angle; sometimes in marks on trees which they had climbed; or in squirrel-traps;* or, which surprised us more, from being new, in decoys for the purpose of ensnaring birds. These are formed of underwood and reeds, long and narrow, shaped like a mound raised over a grave; with a small aperture at one end for admission of the prey; and a grate made of sticks at the other: the bird enters at the aperture, seeing before him the light of the grate, between the bars of which, he vainly endeavours to thrust himself, until taken. Most of these decoys were full of

* A squirrel-trap is a cavity of considerable depth, formed by art, in the body of a tree. When the Indians in their hunting parties set fire to the surrounding country (which is a very common custom) the squirrels, opossums, and other animals, who live in trees, flee for refuge into these holes, whence they are easily dislodged and taken. The natives always pitch on a part of a tree for this purpose, which has been perforated by a worm, which indicates that the wood is in an unsound state, and will readily yield to their efforts. If the rudeness and imperfection of the tools with which they work be considered, it must be confessed to be an operation of great toil and difficulty.

feathers, chiefly those of quails, which shewed their utility. We also met with two old damaged canoes hauled up on the beach, which differed in no wise from those found on the sea coast.

June, 1789. Having remained out three days, we returned to our quarters at Rose-hill, with the pleasing intelligence of our discovery. The country we had passed through we found tolerably plain, and little encumbered with underwood, except near the river side. It is entirely covered with the same sorts of trees as grow near Sydney ; and in some places grass springs up luxuriantly ; other places are quite bare of it. The soil is various: in many parts a stiff arid clay, covered with small pebbles; in other places, of a soft loamy nature: but invariably, in every part near the river, it is a coarse sterile sand. Our observations on it (particulary mine, from carrying the compass by which we steered) were not so numerous as might have been wished. But, certainly, if the qualities of it be such as to deserve future cultivation, no impediment of surface, but that of cutting down and burning the trees, exists, to prevent its being tilled.

To this river the governor gave the name of Nepean. The distance of the part of the river which we first hit upon from the sea coast, is about 39 miles, in a direct line almost due west.

A survey of Botany Bay took place in September. I was of the party, with several other officers. We continued nine days in the bay, during which time, the relative position of every part of it, to the extent of more than thirty miles, following the windings of the shore, was ascertained, and laid down on paper, by captain Hunter.

So complete an opportunity of forming a judgment, enables me to speak decisively of a place, which has often engaged conversation, and excited reflection. Variety of opinions here disappeared. I shall, therefore, transcribe literally what I wrote in my journal, on my return from the expedition.—" We were unanimously of opinion, that had not the nautical part of Mr. Cook's description, in which we include the latitude and longitude of the bay, been so accurately laid down, there would exist the utmost reason to believe, that those who have described the contiguous country, had never seen it. On the sides of the harbour, a line of sea coast more than thirty miles long, we did not find 200 acres which could be cultivated."

September, 1789. But all our attention was not directed to explore inlets, and toil for discovery Our internal tranquillity was still more important. To repress the inroads of depredation; and to secure to honest industry the reward of its labour, had become matter of the most serious consideration ; hardly a night passing without the commission of robbery. Many expedients were devised; and the governor at length determined to select from the convicts, a certain number of persons, who were meant to be of the fairest character, for the purpose of being formed into a nightly-watch, for the preservation of public and private property, under the following regulations, which, as the first system of police in a colony, so peculiarly constituted as ours, may perhaps prove not uninteresting.

I.

" A night-watch, consisting of 12 persons, divided into four
" parties, is appointed, and fully authorized to patrol at all hours
" in the night ; and to visit such places as may be deemed neces-
" sary, for the discovery of any felony, trespass, or misdemeanor;
" and for the apprehending and securing for examination, any
" person or persons who may appear to them concerned therein,
" either by entrance into any suspected hut or dwelling, or by
" such other measure as may seem to them expedient.

II.

" Those parts in which the convicts reside are to be divided and

" numbered, in the following manner.—The convict-huts on the
" eastern side of the stream, and the public farm, are to be the
" first division.—Those at the brick-kilns, and the detached par-
" ties in the different private farms in that district, are to be the
" second division.—Those on the western side of the stream, as
" far as the line which separates the district of the women from
" the men, to be the third division.—The huts occupied from that
" line to the hospital, and from there to the observatory, to be the
" fourth division.

III.

" Each of these districts or divisions is to be under the particular
" inspection of one person, who may be judged qualified to inform
" himself of the actual residence of each individual in his district ;
" as well as of his business, connections, and acquaintances.

IV.

" Cognizance is to be taken of such convicts as may sell or bar-
" ter their slops or provisions ; and also of such as are addicted to
" gaming for either of the aforesaid articles, who are to be reported
" to the judge advocate.

V.

" Any soldier or seaman found straggling after the beating of
" the tattoo ; or who may be found in a convict's hut, is to be de-
" tained ; and information of him immediately given to the nearest
" guard.

VI.

" Any person who may be robbed during the night, is to give
" immediate information thereof to the watch of his district, who,
" on the instant of application being made, shall use the most ef-
" fectual means to trace out the offender, or offenders, so that he,
" she, or they, may be brought to justice.

VII.

" The watch of each district is to be under the direction of one
" person, who will be named for that purpose. All the patrols are
" placed under the immediate inspection of Herbert Keeling They
" are never to receive any fee, gratuity, or reward, from any indi-
" vidual whatever, to engage their exertions in the execution of the
" above trust. Nor will they receive any stipulated encouragement
" for the conviction of any offender. But their diligence and good
" behaviour will be rewarded by the governor. And for this pur-
" pose their conduct will be strictly attended to, by those who are
" placed in authority over them.

VIII.

" The night-watch is to go out as soon as the tattoo ceases beat-
" ing: to return to their huts when the working drum beats in the
" morning: and are to make their report to the judge advocate,
" through Herbert Keeling, of all robberies and misdemeanors
" which may have been committed. Any assistance the patrols
" may require, will be given to them, on applying to the officer
" commanding the nearest guard; and by the civil power, if neces-
" sary; for which last, application is to be made to the provost
" martial.

IX.

" Any negligence on the part of those who shall be employed
" on this duty, will be punished with the utmost rigour of the
" law.

X.

" The night-watch is to consist of 12 persons."

Every political code, either from a defect of its constitution, or
from the corruptness of those who are entrusted to execute it, will

be found less perfect in practice than speculation had promised itself. It were, however, prejudice to deny, that for some time following the institution of this patrol, nightly depredations became less frequent and alarming : the petty villains, at least, were restrained by it. And to keep even a garden unravaged was now become a subject of the deepest concern.

For in October our weekly allowance of provisions, which had hitherto been eight pounds of flour, five pounds of salt pork, three pints of pease, six ounces of butter, was reduced to five pounds five ounces of flour, three pounds five ounces of pork, and two pints of pease.

In order to lessen the consumption from the public stores, the Supply was ordered to touch at Lord Howe Island, in her way from Norfolk Island, to try if turtle could be procured, for the purpose of being publicly served in lieu of salt provisions. But she brought back only three turtles, which were distributed in the garrison.

December, 1789. At the request of his excellency, lieutenant Dawes of the marines, accompanied by lieutenant Johnston and Mr. Lowes, about this time undertook the attempt to cross the Nepean river, and to penetrate to Carmarthen mountains. Having discovered a ford in the river, they passed it, and proceeded in a westerly direction. But they found the country so rugged, and the difficulty of walking so excessive, that in three days they were able to penetrate only fifteen miles : and were therefore obliged to relinquish their object. This party, at the time they turned back, were farther inland than any other persons ever were before or since, being fifty-four miles in a direct line from the sea coast when on the summit of mount Twiss, a hill so named by them, and which bounded their peregrination.

Intercourse with the natives, for the purpose of knowing whe-

F

ther or not the country possessed any resources, by which life might be prolonged,* as well as on other accounts, becoming every day more desirable, the governor resolved to make prisoners of two more of them.

Boats properly provided, under the command of lieutenant Bradley of the Sirius, were accordingly dispatched on this service; and completely succeeded in trepanning and carrying off, without opposition, two fine young men, who were safely landed among us at Sydney.

Nanbaree and Abaroo welcomed them on shore; calling them immediately by their names, Bàn-ee-lon, and Còl-bee. But they seemed little disposed to receive the congratulations, or repose confidence in the assurances of their friends. The same scenes of awkward wonder and impatient constraint, which had attended the introduction of Arabanoo, succeeded. Baneelon we judged to be about twenty-six years old, of good stature, and stoutly made, with a bold intrepid countenance, which bespoke defiance and revenge. Colbee was perhaps near thirty, of a less sullen aspect than his comrade, considerably shorter, and not so robustly framed, though better fitted for purposes of activity. They had both evidently had the small-pox; indeed Colbee's face was very thickly imprinted with the marks of it.

Positive orders were issued by the governor to treat them indulgently, and guard them strictly; notwithstanding which Colbee contrived to effect his escape in about a week, with a small iron ring round his leg. Had those appointed to watch them been a moment later, his companion would have contrived to accompany him.

* One of the convicts, a negro, had twice eloped, with an intention of establishing himself in the society of the natives, with a wish to adopt their customs and to live with them: but he was always repulsed by them; and compelled to return to us from hunger and wretchedness.

But Baneelon, though haughty, knew how to temporize. He quickly threw off all reserve; and pretended, nay, at particular moments, perhaps felt satisfaction in his new state. Unlike poor Arabanoo, he became at once fond of our viands, and would drink the strongest liquors, not simply without reluctance, but with eager marks of delight and enjoyment. He was the only native we ever knew who immediately shewed a fondness for spirits: Colbee would not at first touch them. Nor was the effect of wine or brandy upon him more perceptible than an equal quantity would have produced upon one of us, although fermented liquor was new to him.

In his eating, he was alike compliant. When a turtle was shewn to Arabanoo, he would not allow it to be a fish, and could not be induced to eat of it. Baneelon also denied it to be a fish; but no common councilman in Europe could do more justice than he did to a very fine one, that the Supply had brought from Lord Howe Island, and which was served up at the governor's table on Christmas-day.

His powers of mind were certainly far above mediocrity. He acquired knowledge, both of our manners and language, faster than his predecessor had done. He willingly communicated information; sang, danced, and capered: told us all the customs of his country, and all the details of his family economy. Love and war seemed his favourite pursuits; in both of which he had suffered severely. His head was disfigured by several scars; a spear had passed through his arm, and another through his leg; half of one of his thumbs was carried away; and the mark of a wound appeared on the back of his hand. The cause and attendant circumstances of all these disasters, except one, he related to us. " But " the wound on the back of your hand, Baneelon! how did you get that ?" He laughed, and owned that it was received in carrying off a lady of another tribe by force. " I was dragging her away : " she cried aloud, and stuck her teeth in me."—" And what did " you do then?" " I knocked her down, and beat her till she " was insensible, and covered with blood.—Then"———

Whenever he recounted his battles, " poized his lance, and " shewed how fields were won," the most violent exclamations of rage and vengeance against his competitors in arms, those of the tribe called Cam-ee-ra-gal in particular, would burst from him. And he never failed at such times to solicit the governor to accompany him, with a body of soldiers, in order that he might exterminate this hated name.

Although I call him only Baneelon, he had besides several appellations ; and for a while he chose to be distinguished by that of Wo-lar-a-wàr-ee. Again, as a mark of affection and respect to the governor, he conferred on him the name of Wolarawaree, and sometimes called him *Been-en-a* [father] ; adopting to himself the name of governor. This interchange we found is a constant symbol of friendship among them *. In a word, his temper seemed pliant, and his relish of our society so great, that hardly any one judged he would attempt to quit us, were the means of escape put within his reach. Nevertheless it was thought proper to continue a watch over him.

* It is observable that this custom prevails as a pledge of friendship and kindness all over Asia, and has also been mentioned by Captain Cook to exist among the natives in the South-Sea Islands.

CHAPTER VI.

Transactions of the Colony, from the Beginning of the Year 1790, *until the End of May following.*

Our impatience of news from Europe strongly marked the commencement of the year. We had now been two years in the country, and thirty-two months from England, in which long period no supplies, except what had been procured at the Cape of Good Hope by the Sirius, had reached us. From intelligence of our friends and connections we had been entirely cut off, no communication whatever having passed with our native country since the 13th of May, 1787, the day of our departure from Portsmouth. Famine besides was approaching with gigantic strides, and gloom and dejection overspread every countenance. Men abandoned themselves to the most desponding reflections, and adopted the most extravagant conjectures.

Still we were on the tiptoe of expectation. If thunder broke at a distance, or a fowling-piece of louder than ordinary report resounded in the woods, " *a gun from a ship,*" was echoed on every side, and nothing but hurry and agitation prevailed. For eighteen months after we had landed in the country, a party of marines used to go weekly to Botany Bay, to see whether any vessel, ignorant of our removal to Port Jackson, might be arrived there. But a better plan was now devised, on the suggestion of captain Hunter. A party of seamen were fixed on a high bluff, called the South-head, at the entrance of the harbour, on which a flag was ordered to be hoisted, whenever a ship might appear, which should serve as a direction to her, and as a signal of approach to us. Every officer stepped forward to volunteer a service which promised to be so replete with beneficial consequences. But the zeal and alacrity of captain Hunter, and our brethren of the Sirius, rendered superfluous all assistance or co-operation.

1790. Here on the summit of the hill, every morning from daylight until the sun sunk, did we sweep the horizon, in hope of seeing a sail. At every fleeting speck which arose from the bosom of the sea, the heart bounded, and the telescope was lifted to the eye. If a ship appeared here, we knew she must be bound to us; for on the shores of this vast ocean (the largest in the world) we were the only community which possessed the art of navigation, and languished for intercourse with civilized society.

To say that we were disappointed and shocked, would very inadequately describe our sensations. But the misery and horror of such a situation cannot be imparted, even by those who have suffered under it.

March, 1790. Vigorous measures were become indispensable. The governor therefore, early in February, ordered the Sirius to prepare for a voyage to China; and a farther retrenchment of our ration, we were given to understand, would take place on her sailing.

But the Sirius was destined not to reach China. Previously to her intended departure on that voyage, she was ordered, in concert with the Supply, to convey major Ross, with a large detachment of marines, and more than two hundred convicts, to Norfolk

Island : it being hoped that such a division of our numbers would increase the means of subsistence, by diversified exertions She sailed on the 6th of March. And on the 27th of the same month, the following order was issued from head quarters.

" Parole   —   Honour.

" Counter sign   —   Example.

" The expected supply of provisions not having arrived, makes " it necessary to reduce the present ration. And the commissary " is directed to issue, from the 1st of April, the undermentioned " allowance, to every person in the settlement without distinc- " tion.

" Four pounds of flour, two pounds and a half of salt pork, " and one pound and a half of rice, per week."

On the 5th of April news was brought, that the flag on the South-head was hoisted. Less emotion was created by the news than might be expected ; every one coldly said to his neighbour, " the Sirius and Supply are returned from Norfolk Island." To satisfy myself that the flag was really flying, I went to the observatory, and looked for it through the large astronomical telescope, when I plainly saw it. But I was immediately convinced that it was not to announce the arrival of ships from England ; for I could see nobody near the flag-staff except one solitary being, who kept strolling around, unmoved by what he saw. I well knew how different an effect the sight of strange ships would produce.

April, 1790. The governor, however, determined to go down the harbour, and I begged permission to accompany him. Having turned a point about half way down, we were surprised to see a boat, which was known to belong to the Supply, rowing towards us. On nearer approach, I saw captain Ball make an extraordinary motion with his hand, which too plainly indicated that something disastrous had happened ; and I could not help turn-

ing to the governor, near whom I sat, and saying, " Sir, pre-
" pare yourself for bad news." A few minutes changed doubt
into certainty ; and to our unspeakable consternation we learned,
that the Sirius had been wrecked on Norfolk Island, on the 19th
of February. Happily, however, captain Hunter, and every
other person belonging to her, were saved.

Dismay was painted on every countenance, when the tidings
were proclaimed at Sydney. The most distracting apprehensions
were entertained ; all hopes were now concentred in the little
Supply.

At six o'clock in the evening, all the officers of the garrison,
both civil and military, were summoned to meet the governor in
council ; when the nature of our situation was fully discussed ;
and an account of the provisions yet remaining in store laid before
the council by the commissary. This account stated, that on the
present ration * the public stores contained salt meat sufficient to
serve until the 2d of July ; flour until the 20th of August ; and
rice, or pease in lieu of it, until the 1st of October.

Several regulations for the more effectual preservation of gardens, and other private property, were proposed, and adopted :
and after some interchange of opinion, the following ration was
decreed to commence immediately : a vigorous exertion to prolong existence, or the chance of relief, being all now left to us.

" Two pounds of pork, two pounds and a half of flour, two
" pounds of rice, or a quart of pease, per week, to every grown
" person, and to every child of more than eighteen months old."

" To every child under eighteen months old, the same quantity
of rice and flour, and one pound of pork †.

* See the ration of the 27th of March, a few pages back.

† When the age of this provision is recollected, its inadequacy will more strikingly appear. The pork and rice were brought with us from England : the pork had been salted
between three and four years, and every grain of rice was a moving body, from the inhabi-

The immediate departure of the Supply, for Batavia, was also determined.

Nor did our zeal stop here. The governor being resolved to employ all the boats, public and private, in procuring fish, which was intended to be served in lieu of salt malt, all the officers, civil and military, including the clergyman, and the surgeons of the hospital, made the voluntary offer, in addition to their other duties, to go alternately every night in these boats, in order to see that every exertion was made; and that all the fish which might be caught was deposited with the commissary.

The best marksmen of the marines and convicts were also selected, and put under the command of a trusty serjeant, with directions to range the woods in search of kanguroos; which were ordered, when brought in, to be delivered to the commissary.

And as it was judged that the inevitable fatigues of shooting and fishing could not be supported on the common ration, a small additional quantity of flour and pork was appropriated to the use of the gamekeepers ; and each fisherman, who had been out during the preceding night had, on his return in the morning, a pound of uncleaned fish allowed for his breakfast.

April, 1790. On the 17th instant, the Supply, captain Ball, sailed for Batavia. We followed her with anxious eyes until she was no longer visible. Truly did we say to her—" *In te omnis* " *domus inclinata recumbit.*" We were, however, consoled by re-

tants lodged within it. We soon left off boiling the pork, as it had become so old and dry, that it shrunk one half in its dimensions when so dressed. Our usual method of cooking it was to cut off the daily morsel, and toast it on a fork before the fire, catching the drops which fell on a slice of bread, or in a saucer of rice. Our flour was the remnant of what was brought from the Cape, by the Sirius, and was good. Instead of baking it, the soldiers and convicts used to boil it up with greens.

G

flecting, that every thing which zeal, fortitude, and seamanship, could produce, was concentred in her commander.

Our bosoms consequently became less perturbed ; and all our labour and attention were turned on one object—the procuring of food —" Pride, pomp, and circumstance of glorious war were " no more."

The distress of the lower classes for clothes was almost equal to their other wants. The stores had been long exhausted, and winter was at hand. Nothing more ludicrous can be conceived than the expedients of substituting, shifting, and patching, which ingenuity devised, to eke out wretchedness, and preserve the remains of decency. The superior dexterity of the women was particularly conspicuous. Many a guard have I seen mount, in which the number of soldiers without shoes, exceeded that which had yet preserved remnants of leather.

Nor was another part of our domestic economy less whimsical. If a lucky man, who had knocked down a dinner with his gun, or caught a fish by angling from the rocks, invited a neighbour to dine with him, the invitation always ran, " bring your own " bread." Even at the governor's table, this custom was constantly observed. Every man when he sat down pulled his bread out of his pocket, and laid it by his plate.

The insufficiency of our ration soon diminished our execution of labour. Both soldiers and convicts pleaded such loss of strength, as to find themselves unable to perform their accustomed tasks. The hours of public work were accordingly shortened ; or rather, every man was ordered to do as much as his strength would permit ; and every other possible indulgence was granted.

May, 1790. In proportion, however, as lenity and mitigation were extended to inability and helplessness, inasmuch was the

most rigorous justice executed on disturbers of the public tranquillity. Persons detected in robbing gardens, or pilfering provisions, were never screened : because as every man could possess, by his utmost exertions, but a bare sufficiency to preserve life,* he who deprived his neighbour of that little, drove him to desperation. No new laws for the punishment of theft were enacted ; but persons of all descriptions were publicly warned, that the severest penalties, which the existing law in its greatest latitude would authorise, should be inflicted on offenders. The following sentence of a court of justice, of which I was a member, on a convict detected in a garden stealing potatoes, will illustrate the subject —" He was ordered to receive three hundred lashes imme-
" diately, to be chained for six months to two other criminals, who
" were thus fettered for former offences, and to have his allowance
" of flour stopped for six months."—So that during the operation of the sentence, two pounds of pork, and two pounds of rice (or in lieu of the latter, a quart of pease) per week, constituted his whole subsistence. Such was the melancholy length to which we were compelled to stretch our penal system.

Farther to contribute to the detection of villainy, a proclamation, offering a reward of sixty pounds of flour, more tempting than the ore of Peru or Potosi, was promised to any one who should apprehend, and bring to justice, a robber of garden ground.

Our friend Baneelon, during this season of scarcity, was as well taken care of as our desperate circumstances would allow. We

* Its preservation in some cases was found impracticable. Three or four instances of persons who perished from want have been related to me. One only, however, fell within my own observation —I was passing the provision-store, when a man, with a wild haggard countenance, who had just received his daily pittance to carry home, came out. His faltering gait, and eager devouring eye, led me to watch him; and he had not proceeded ten steps before he fell. I ordered him to be carried to the hospital, where, when he arrived, he was found dead. On opening the body, the cause of death was pronounced to be *inanition*.

knew not how to keep him, and yet were unwilling to part with him. Had he penetrated our state, perhaps he might have given his countrymen such a description of our diminished numbers, and diminished strength, as would have emboldened them to become more troublesome. Every expedient was used to keep him in ignorance; his allowance was regularly received by the governor's servant, like that of any other person ; but the ration of a week was insufficient to have kept him for a day; the deficiency was supplied by fish, whenever it could be procured, and a little Indian corn, which had been reserved, was ground and appropriated to his use. In spite of all these aids, want of food has been known to make him furious, and often melancholy.

May, 1790. There is reason to believe that he had long meditated his escape, which he effected in the night of the 3d instant. About two o'clock in the morning, he pretended illness, and awaking the servant who lay in the room with him, begged to go down stairs. The other attended him without suspicion of his design ; and Baneelon no sooner found himself in a back-yard, than he nimbly leaped over a slight paling, and bade us adieu.

The following public order was issued within the date of this chapter, and is too pleasing a proof that universal depravity did not prevail among the convicts, to be omitted.

" The governor, in consequence of the unremitted good beha-
" viour and meritorious conduct of John Irving, is pleased to re-
" mit the remainder of the term for which he was sentenced to
" transportation. He is therefore to be considered as restored to
" all those rights and privileges, which had been suspended in
" consequence of the sentence of the law. And as such, he is
" hereby appointed to act as an assistant to the surgeon at Nor-
" folk Island."

CHAPTER VII.

Transactions of the Colony in June, July, and August, 1790.

June. At length the clouds of misfortune began to separate, and on the evening of the 3d of June, the joyful cry of " the flag's " up," resounded in every direction.

I was sitting in my hut, musing on our fate, when a confused clamour in the street drew my attention. I opened my door, and saw several women with children in their arms running to and fro with distracted looks, congratulating each other, and kissing their infants with the most passionate and extravagant marks of fondness. I needed no more ; but instantly started out, and ran to a hill, where, by the assistance of a pocket-glass, my hopes were realized. My next door neighbour, a brother-officer, was with me ; but we could not speak ; we wrung each other by the hand, with eyes and hearts overflowing.

Finding that the governor intended to go immediately in his boat down the harbour, I begged to be of his party.

As we proceeded, the object of our hopes soon appeared :—a large ship, with English colours flying, working in, between the heads which form the entrance of the harbour. The tumultuous state of our minds represented her in danger ; and we were in agony. Soon after, the governor, having ascertained what she was, left us, and stept into a fishing boat to return to Sydney. The weather was wet and tempestuous ;

but the body is delicate only when the soul is at ease. We pushed through wind and rain, the anxiety of our sensations every moment redoubling. At last we read the word *London* on her stern. " Pull away, my lads! she is from Old England! a few strokes " more, and we shall be aboard! hurrah for a belly-full, and news " from our friends!"—Such were our exhortations to the boat's crew.

A few minutes completed our wishes, and we found ourselves on board the Lady Juliana transport, with two hundred and twenty-five of our countrywomen, whom crime or misfortune had condemned to exile. We learned that they had been almost eleven months on their passage, having left Plymouth, into which port they had put in July, 1789. We continued to ask a thousand questions on a breath. Stimulated by curiosity, they inquired in turn; but the right of being first answered, we thought, lay on our side. " Letters! letters!" was the cry. They were produced, and torn open in trembling agitation. News burst upon us like meridian splendor on a blind man. We were overwhelmed with it; public, private, general, and particular. Nor was it until some days had elapsed, that we were able to methodize it, or reduce it into form. We now heard for the first time of our sovereign's illness, and his happy restoration to health. The French revolution * of 1789, with all the attendant circum-

---

* These words bring to my mind an anecdote, which, though rather out of place, I shall offer no apology for introducing.—Among other inquiries, we were anxious to learn whether M. de la Peyrouse, with the two ships under his command, bound on a voyage of discovery, had arrived in France. We heard with concern, that no accounts of them had been received, since they had left Botany Bay, in March, 1788. I remember when they were at that place, one day conversing with Monsieur de la Peyrouse, about the best method of treating savage people, " Sir," said he, " I have sometimes been compelled to commit hostilities upon " them, but never without suffering the most poignant regret ; for, independent of my own " feelings on the occasion, his Majesty's (Louis XVI.) last words to me, *de sa propre bouche,*

stances of that wonderful and unexpected event, succeeded to amaze us. Now, too, the disaster which had befallen the Guardian, and the liberal and enlarged plan on which she had been stored and fitted out by government for our use, was promulged. It served also, in some measure, to account why we had not sooner heard from England. For had not the Guardian struck on an island of ice, she would probably have reached us three months before, and in this case have prevented the loss of the Sirius, although she had sailed from England three months after the Lady Juliana.

June, 1790. A general thanksgiving to Almighty God, for his Majesty's recovery, and happy restoration to his family and subjects, was ordered to be offered up on the following Wednesday, when all public labour was suspended ; and every person in the settlement attended at church, where a sermon, suited to an occasion, at once so full of gratitude and solemnity, was preached by the Reverend Richard Johnson, chaplain of the colony.

All the officers were afterwards entertained at dinner by the governor. And in the evening, an address to his excellency, expressive of congratulation and loyalty, was agreed upon ; and in two days after was presented, and very graciously received.

The following invitation to the non-commissioned officers and private soldiers of the marine battalion, was also about this time published.

" In consequence of the assurance that was given to the non-
" commissioned officers and men belonging to the battalion of
" marines, on their embarking for the service of this country, that
" such of them as should behave well, would be allowed to quit

---

" when I took leave of him at Versailles, were—It is my express injunction, that you always
" treat the Indian nations with kindness and humanity ; gratify their wishes, and never,
" but in a case of the last necessity, when self-defence requires it, shed human blood."—
Are these the sentiments of a tyrant, of a sanguinary and perfidious man ?

" the service, on their return to England; or be discharged
" abroad, upon the relief taking place, and permitted to settle
" in the country.—His Majesty has been graciously pleased to di-
" rect the following encouragement to be held up to such non-
" commissioned officers and privates, as may be disposed to become
" settlers in this country, or in any of the islands comprized within
" the government of the continent of New South Wales, on the
" arrival of the corps raised and intended for the service of this
" colony, and for their relief, viz.

" To every non-commissioned officer, an allotment of one
" hundred and thirty acres of land, if single, and of one hundred
" and fifty acres, if married. To every private soldier, an allot-
" ment of eighty acres, if single, and of one hundred acres, if
" married; and also an allotment of ten acres for every child,
" whether of a non-commissioned officer, or of a private soldier.
" These allotments will be free of all fines, taxes, quit-rents, and
" other acknowledgments, for the space of ten years; but after
" the expiration of that period, will be subject to an annual quit-
" rent of one shilling for every fifty acres.

" His Majesty has likewise been farther pleased to signify his
" royal will and pleasure, that a bounty of three pounds be of-
" fered to each non-commissioned officer and soldier, who may
" be disposed to continue in this country, and inlist in the corps
" appointed for the service of New South Wales; with a farther
" assurance, that in case of a proper demeanour on their part,
" they shall, after a farther service of five years, be entitled to
" double the former portion of land, provided they then choose to
" become settlers in the country, free of all taxes, fines, and quit-
" rents, for the space of fifteen years; but after that time, to be
" subject to the beforementioned annual quit-rent of one shilling
" for every fifty acres.

" And as a farther encouragement to those men who may be de-
" sirous to become settlers, and continue in the country, his Ma-
" jesty has been likewise pleased to direct, that every man shall,
" on being discharged, receive out of the public store, a portion
" of clothing and provisions, sufficient for his support for one
" year ; together with a suitable quantity of seeds, grain, &c.
" for the tillage of the land ; and a portion of tools and imple-
" ments of agriculture, proper for their use. And whenever any
" man, who may become a settler, can maintain, feed, and clothe,
" such number of convicts as may be judged necessary by the go-
" vernor, for the time being, to assist him in clearing and culti-
" vating the land, the service of such convicts shall be assigned to
" him."

June, 1790. We were joyfully surprised on the 20th of the
month to see another sail enter the harbour. She proved to be
the Justinian transport, commanded by captain Maitland ; and
our rapture was doubled.on finding that she was laden entirely
with provisions for our use. Full allowance, and general congratulation, immediately took place. This ship had left Falmouth
on the preceding 20th of January, and completed her passage exactly in five months*. She had staid at Madeira one day, and
four at Saint Jago ; from which last place she had steered directly
for New South Wales, neglecting Rio de Janeiro on her right,

---

* Accident only prevented her from making it in eighteen days less; for she was then in
sight of the harbour's mouth, when an unpropitious gale of wind blew her off; otherwise
she would have reached us one day sooner than the Lady Juliana.—It is a curious circumstance, that these two ships had sailed together from the river Thames, one bound to Port
Jackson, and the other bound to Jamaica. The Justinian carried her cargo to the last
mentioned place, landed it; and loaded afresh with sugars, which she returned with, and
delivered in London. She was then hired as a transport, reladen, and sailed for New South
Wales. Let it be remembered, that no material accident had happened to either vessel.
But what will not zeal and diligence accomplish !

H

and the Cape of Good Hope on her left; and notwithstanding the immense tract of ocean she had passed, brought her crew without sickness into harbour. When the novelty and boldness of such an attempt shall be recollected, too much praise, on the spirit and activity of Mr. Maitland, cannot be bestowed.

June, 1790. Good fortune continued to befriend us. Before the end of the month, three more transports, having on board two companies of the New South Wales corps, arrived to add to our society. These ships also brought out a large body of convicts, whose state and sufferings will be best estimated by the following return.

Names of the Ships.	Number of people embarked.	Number of persons who died on the passage.	Number landed sick at Port Jackson.
Neptune	530	163	269
Surprise	252	42	121
Scarborough	256	68	96
	1038	273	486

N. B. Of those landed sick, one hundred and twenty-four died in the hospital at Sydney.

On our passage from England, which had lasted more than eight months, and with nearly an equal number of persons, only twenty-four had died, and not thirty were landed sick. The difference can be accounted for, only by comparing the manner in which each fleet was fitted out and conducted. With us the provisions, served on board, were laid in by a contractor, who sent a deputy to serve them out ; and it became a part of duty for the officers of the troops to inspect their quality, and to order that every one received his just proportion. Whereas, in the fleet now arrived, the distribution of provisions rested entirely with the masters of the merchantmen, and the officers were expressly forbidden to interfere in any shape farther about the convicts than to prevent their escape.

Seventeen pounds, in full of all expence, was the sum paid by the public for the passage of each person. And this sum was certainly competent to afford fair profit to the merchant who contracted. But there is reason to believe, that some of those who were employed to act for him, violated every principle of justice, and rioted on the spoils of misery, for want of a controlling power to check their enormities. No doubt can be entertained, that a humane and liberal government will interpose its authority, to prevent the repetition of such flagitious conduct.

Although the convicts had landed from these ships with every mark of meagre misery, yet it was soon seen, that a want of room, in which more conveniences might have been stowed for their use, had not caused it. Several of the masters of the transports inmediately opened stores, and exposed large quantities of goods to sale, which, though at most extortionate prices, were eagerly bought up.

Such was the weakly state of the new comers, that for several weeks little real benefit to the colony was derived from so great a nominal addition to our number. However, as fast as they recovered, employment was immediately assigned to them. The old hours of labour, which had been reduced in our distress, were re-established, and the most vigorous measures adopted to give prosperity to the settlement. New buildings were immediately planned ; and large tracts of ground, at Rose-hill, ordered to be cleared, and prepared for cultivation. Some superintendants who had arrived in the fleet, and were hired by government for the purpose of overlooking and directing the convicts, were found extremely serviceable in accelerating the progress of improvement.

July, 1790. This month was marked by nothing worth communication, except a melancholy accident which befel a young gentleman of amiable character, one of the midshipmen lately belonging to the Sirius, and two marines. He was in a small boat, with three marines, in the harbour, when a whale was seen near them. Sensible of their danger, they used every effort to avoid the cause of it, by rowing in a contrary direction from that which the fish seemed to take ; but the monster suddenly arose close to them, and nearly filled the boat with water. By exerting themselves, they baled her out, and again steered from it. For some time it was not seen, and they conceived themselves safe, when, rising immediately under the boat, it lifted her to the height of many yards on its back, whence slipping off, she dropped as from a precipice, and immediately filled and sunk. The midshipman and one of the marines were sucked into the vortex which the whale had made, and disappeared at once. The two other marines swam for the nearest shore ; but one only reached it, to recount the fate of his companions.

August, 1790. In the beginning of this month, in company with Mr. Dawes and Mr. Worgan, late surgeon of the Sirius, I undertook an expedition to the southward and westward of Rose-hill, where the country had never been explored. We remained out seven days, and penetrated to a considerable distance in a S.S.W. direction, bounding our course at a remarkable hill, to which, from its conical shape, we gave the name of Pyramid-hill. Except the discovery of a river (which is unquestionably the Nepean near its source) to which we gave the name of the Worgan, in honour of one of our party, nothing very interesting was remarked.

Towards the end of the month, we made a second excursion to the north-west of Rose-hill, when we again fell in with the Nepean, and traced it to the spot where it had been first discovered by the party of which I was a member, fourteen months before; examining the country as we went along. Little doubt now subsisted that the Hawkesbury and Nepean were one river.

We undertook a third expedition soon after to Broken Bay; which place we found had not been exaggerated in description, whether its capacious harbour, or its desolate incultivable shores, be considered.—On all these excursions we brought away, in small bags, as many specimens of the soil of the country we had passed through, as could be conveniently carried; in order that by analysis its qualities might be ascertained.

CHAPTER VIII.

Transactions of the Colony in the Beginning of September, 1790.

THE tremendous monster, who had occasioned the unhappy catastrophe just recorded, was fated to be the cause of farther mischief to us.

September, 1790. On the 7th instant, captain Nepean, of the New South Wales corps, and Mr. White, accompanied by little Nanbaree, and a party of men, went in a boat to Manly Cove, intending to land there, and walk on to Broken Bay. On drawing near the shore, a dead whale, in the most disgusting state of putrefaction, was seen lying on the beach, and at least two hundred Indians surrounding it, broiling the flesh on different fires, and feasting on it with the most extravagant marks of greediness and rapture. As the boat continued to approach, they were observed to fall into confusion, and to pick up their spears; on which our people lay upon their oars: and Nanbaree stepping forward, harangued them for some time, assuring them that we were friends. Mr. White now called for Baneelon; who, on hearing his name, came forth, and entered into conversation. He was greatly emaciated, and so far disfigured by a long beard, that our people not without difficulty recognized their old acquaintance. His answering in broken English, and inquiring for the governor, however, soon corrected their doubts. He seemed quite friendly. And soon after Colbee came up, pointing to his leg, to shew that he had freed himself from the fetter which was upon him, when he had escaped from us.

When Baneelon was told that the governor was not far off, he expressed great joy, and declared that he would immediately go in search of him; and if he found him not, would follow him to Sydney. " Have you brought any hatchets with you?" cried he. Unluckily they had not any which they chose to spare; but two or three shirts, some handkerchiefs, knives, and other trifles, were given to them, and seemed to satisfy. Baneelon, willing to instruct his countrymen, tried to put on a shirt, but managed it so awkwardly, that a man of the name of M'Entire, the governor's gamekeeper, was directed by Mr. White to assist him. This man, who was well known to him, he positively forbade to approach, eyeing him ferociously, and with every mark of horror and resentment. He was in consequence left to himself, and the conversation proceeded as before. The length of his beard seemed to annoy him much, and he expressed eager wishes to be shaved, asking repeatedly for a razor. A pair of scissors was given to him, and he shewed he had not forgotten how to use such an instrument, for he forthwith began to clip his hair with it.

During this time, the women and children, to the number of more than fifty, stood at a distance, and refused all invitations, which could be conveyed by signs and gestures, to approach nearer. " Which of them is your old favourite, Bar-an-gar-oo, of " whom you used to speak so often?"—" Oh," said he, " she is " become the wife of Colbee! but I have got *Bul-la Mur-ree Dee-in* [two large women] to compensate for her loss."

September, 1790. It was observed that he had received two wounds, in addition to his former numerous ones, since he had left us; one of them from a spear, which had passed through the fleshy part of his arm; and the other displayed itself in a large scar above his left eye. They were both healed, and probably were acquired in the conflict wherein he had asserted his pretensions to the two ladies.

Nanbaree, all this while, though he continued to interrogate his countrymen, and to interpret on both sides, shewed little desire to return to their society, and stuck very close to his new friends. On being asked the cause of their present meeting, Baneelon pointed to the whale, which stunk immoderately; and Colbee made signals, that it was common among them to eat until the stomach was so overladen as to occasion sickness.

Their demand of hatchets being re-iterated, notwithstanding our refusal; they were asked why they had not brought with them some of their own? They excused themselves by saying, that on an occasion of the present sort, they always left them at home, and cut up the whale with the shell which is affixed to the end of the throwing-stick.

Our party now thought it time to proceed on their original expedition, and having taken leave of their sable friends, rowed to some distance, where they landed, and set out for Broken Bay, ordering the coxswain of the boat, in which they had come down, to go immediately and acquaint the governor of all that had passed. When the natives saw that the boat was about to depart, they crowded around her, and brought down, by way of present, three or four great junks of the whale, and put them on board of her; the largest of which, Baneelon expressly requested might be offered, in his name, to the governor.

It happened that his excellency had this day gone to a land-mark, which was building on the South-head, near the flag-staff, to serve as a direction to ships at sea; and the boat met him on his return to Sydney. Immediately on receiving the intelligence, he hastened back to the South-head, and having procured all the fire-arms which could be mustered there, consisting of four mus-kets and a pistol, set out, attended by Mr. Collins and lieutenant Waterhouse of the navy.

September, 1790. When the boat reached Manly Cove, the natives were found still busily employed around the whale. As they expressed not any consternation on seeing us row to the beach, governor Phillip stepped out unarmed, and attended by one seaman only, and called for Baneelon, who appeared, but, notwithstanding his former eagerness, would not suffer the other to approach him for several minutes. Gradually, however, he warmed into friendship and frankness, and presently after Colbee came up. They discoursed for some time, Baneelon expressing pleasure to see his old acquaintance, and inquiring by name for every person whom he could recollect at Sydney ; and among others for a French cook, one of the governor's servants, whom he had constantly made the butt of his ridicule, by mimicking his voice, gait, and other peculiarities, all of which he again went through with his wonted exactness and drollery. He asked also particularly for a lady from whom he had once ventured to snatch a kiss ; and on being told that she was well, by way of proving that the token was fresh in his remembrance, he kissed lieutenant Waterhouse, and laughed aloud. On his wounds being noticed, he coldly said, that he had received them at Botany Bay, but went no farther into their history.

September, 1790. Hatchets still continued to be called for with redoubled eagerness, which rather surprized us, as formerly they had always been accepted with indifference. But Baneelon had probably demonstrated to them their superiority over those of their own manufacturing. To appease their importunity, the governor gave them a knife, some bread, pork, and other articles ; and promised that in two days he would return hither, and bring

I

with him hatchets to be distributed among them, which appeared to diffuse general satisfaction.

Baneelon's love of wine has been mentioned; and the governor, to try whether it still subsisted, uncorked a bottle, and poured out a glass of it, which the other drank off with his former marks of relish and good humour, giving for a toast, as he had been taught, " *the King*."

Our party now advanced from the beach; but perceiving many of the Indians filing off to the right and left, so as in some measure to surround them, they retreated gently to their old situation, which produced neither alarm or offence; the others by degrees also resumed their former position. A very fine barbed spear of uncommon size being seen by the governor, he asked for it. But Baneelon, instead of complying with the request, took it away, and laid it at some distance, and brought back a throwing-stick, which he presented to his excellency.

Matters had proceeded in this friendly train for more than half an hour, when a native, with a spear in his hand, came forward, and stopped at the distance of between twenty and thirty yards from the place where the governor, Mr. Collins, lieutenant Waterhouse, and a seaman stood. His excellency held out his hand, and called to him, advancing towards him at the same time, Mr. Collins following close behind. He appeared to be a man of middle age, short of stature, sturdy, and well set, seemingly a stranger, and but little acquainted with Baneelon and Colbee. The nearer, the governor approached, the greater became the terror and agitation of the Indian. To remove his fear, governor Phillip threw down a dirk, which he wore at his side. The other, alarmed at the rattle of the dirk, and probably misconstruing the action, instantly fixed his lance in his throwing-stick *. To retreat, his excellency now thought would be more dangerous than to advance. He therefore cried out to the man, *Weè-ree, Weè-ree*, (bad ; you are doing wrong) displaying at the same time, every token of amity and confidence. The words had, however, hardly gone forth, when the Indian, stepping back with one foot, aimed his lance with such force and dexterity, that striking † the governor's right shoulder, just above the collar-bone, the point glancing downward, came out at his back, having made a wound of many inches long. The man was observed to keep his eye steadily fixed on the lance until it struck its object, when he directly dashed into the woods and was seen no more.

Instant confusion on both sides took place ; Baneelon and Colbee disappeared ; and several spears were thrown from different quarters, though without effect. Our party retreated as fast as they could, calling to those who were left in the boat, to hasten up with fire-arms. A situation more distressing than that of the governor, during the time that this lasted, cannot readily be conceived :—the pole of the spear, not less than ten feet in length, sticking out before him, and impeding his flight, the butt frequently striking the ground, and lacerating the wound. In vain did Mr. Waterhouse try to break it ; and the barb, which appeared on the other side, forbade extraction, until that could be performed. At length it was broken, and his excellency reached the boat, by which time the seamen with the musquets had got up, and were endeavouring to fire them, but one only would go off, and there is no room to believe that it was attended with any execution.

* Such preparation is equal to what cocking a gun, and directing it at its object, would be with us. To launch the spear, or to touch the trigger, only remains.

† His excellency described the shock to me as similar to a violent blow, with such energy was the weapon thrown.

When the governor got home, the wound was examined: it had bled a good deal in the boat, and it was doubtful whether the subclavian artery might not be divided. On moving the spear, it was found, however, that it might be safely extracted, which was accordingly performed.

Apprehension for the safety of the party who had gone to Broken Bay, now took place. Lieutenant Long, with a detachment of marines, was immediately sent to escort them back, lest any ambush might be laid by the natives to cut them off. When Mr. Long reached Manly Cove, the sun had set; however, he pursued his way in the dark, scrambling over rocks and thickets, as well as he could, until two o'clock on the following morning, when he overtook them at a place where they had halted to sleep, about half-way between the two harbours.

At day-break they all returned, and were surprised to find tracks in the sand of the feet of the Indians, almost the whole way from the place where they had slept to the Cove. By this it should seem as if these last had secretly followed them, probably with hostile intentions; but on discovering their strength, and that they were on their guard, had abandoned their design.

On reaching Manly Cove, three Indians were observed standing on a rock, with whom they entered into conversation. The Indians informed them, that the man who had wounded the governor, belonged to a tribe residing at Broken Bay, and they seemed highly to condemn what he had done. Our gentlemen asked them for a spear, which they immediately gave. The boat's crew said that Baneelon and Colbee had just departed, after a friendly intercourse: like the others, they had pretended highly to disapprove the conduct of the man who had thrown the spear, vowing to execute vengeance upon him.

September, 1790. From this time, until the 14th, no communication passed between the natives and us. On that day, the chaplain and lieutenant Dawes, having Abaroo with them in a boat, learned from two Indians that Wil-ee-ma-rin was the name of the person who had wounded the governor. These two people inquired kindly hcw his excellency did, and seemed pleased to hear that he was likely to recover. They said that they were inhabitants of Rose Hill, and expressed great dissatisfaction at the number of white men who had settled in their former territories. In consequence of which declaration, the detachment at that post was reinforced on the following day.

September, 1790. A hazardous enterprize (but when liberty is the stake, what enterprize is too hazardous for its attainment!) was undertaken in this month by five convicts at Rose Hill, who, in the night, seized a small punt there, and proceeded in her to the South-head, whence they seized and carried off a boat, appropriated to the use of the look-out-house, and put to sea in her, doubtless with a view of reaching any port they could arrive at, and asserting their freedom. They had all come out in the last fleet; and for some time previous to their elopement, had been collecting fishing tackle, and hoarding up provisions, to enable them to put their scheme into execution. *

* They have never since been heard of. Before they went away, they tried in vain to procure fire-arms. If they were not swallowed by the sea, probably they were cut off by the natives, on some part of the coast where their necessities obliged them to land.

CHAPTER. IX.

Transactions of the Colony in part of September and October, 1790.

September, 1790. FROM so unfavourable an omen as I have just related, who could prognosticate that an intercourse with the natives was about to commence ! that the foundation of what neither entreaty, munificence, or humanity, could induce, should be laid by a deed, which threatened to accumulate scenes of bloodshed and horror, was a consequence which neither speculation could predict, or hope expect to see accomplished.

On the 15th a fire being seen on the north shore of the harbour, a party of our people went thither, accompanied by Nanbaree and Abaroo; they found there Baneelon, and several other natives, and much civility passed, which was cemented by a mutal promise to meet in the afternoon at the same place. Both sides were punctual to their engagement, and no objection being made to our landing, a party of us went ashore to them unarmed. Several little presents, which had been purposely brought, were distributed among them; and to Baneelon were given a hatchet and a fish. At a distance stood some children, who, though at first timorous and unwilling to approach, were soon persuaded to advance, and join the men. A bottle of wine was produced, and Baneelon immediately prepared for the charge. Bread and beef he called loudly for, which were given to him, and he began to eat, offering a part of his fare to his countrymen, two of whom tasted the beef, but none of them

would touch the bread Having finished his repast, he made a
motion to be shaved, and a barber being present, his request was
complied with, to the great admiration of his countrymen, who
laughed and exclaimed at the operation. They would not, however, consent to undergo it, but suffered their beards to be clipped
with a pair of scissars. On being asked where their women were,
they pointed to the spot, but seemed not desirous that we should
approach it. However, in a few minutes, a female appeared not
far off, and Abaroo was dispatched to her. Baneelon now joined
with Abaroo to persuade her to come to us, telling us she was Barangaroo, and his wife, notwithstanding he had so lately pretended
that she had left him for Colbee. At length she yielded, and Abaroo, having first put a *petticoat* on her, brought her to us. But this
was the prudery of the wilderness, which her husband joined us to
ridicule, and we soon laughed her out of it. The petticoat was
dropped with hesitation, and Barangaroo stood " armed cap-a-
" pee in nakedness." At the request of Baneelon, we combed and
cut her hair, and she seemed pleased with the operation. Wine
she would not taste, but turned from it with disgust, though
heartily invited to drink by the example and persuasion of Baneelon. In short, she behaved so well, and assumed the character of
gentleness and timidity to such advantage, that had our acquaintance ended here, a very moderate share of the spirit of travelling
would have sufficed to record, that amidst a horde of roaming savages, in the desert wastes of New South Wales, might be found as
much feminine innocence, softness, and modesty (allowing for inevitable difference of education), as the most finished system could
bestow, or the most polished circle produce. So little fitted are
we to judge of human nature at once! And yet on such grounds have
countries been described, and nations characterized. Hence have
arisen those speculative and laborious compositions on the advan-

tages and superiority of a state of nature.—But to resume my subject.

September, 1790. Supposing, that by a private conversation, she might be induced to visit Sydney, which would be the means of drawing her husband and others thither; Abaroo was instructed to take her aside, and try if she could persuade her to comply with our wish. They wandered away together accordingly; but it was soon seen, that Barangaroo's arguments to induce Abaroo to rejoin their society, were more powerful than those of the latter, to prevail upon her to come among us; for it was not without manifest reluctance, and often repeated injunctions, that Abaroo would quit her countrywomen: and when she had done so, she sat in the boat, in sullen silence, evidently occupied by reflection on the scene she had left behind, and returning inclination to her former habits of life.

Nor was a circumstance which had happened in the morning interview, perhaps, wholly unremembered by the girl: we had hinted to Baneelon to provide a husband for her, who should be at liberty to pass and repass to and from Sydney, as he might chuse. There was at the time, a slender fine looking youth in company, called Im-ee-ra-wan-yee, about sixteen years old. The lad, on being invited, came immediately up to her, and offered many blandishments, which proved that he had assumed the *toga virilis*. But Abaroo disclaimed his advances, repeating the name of another person, who we knew was her favourite. The young lover was not, however, easily repulsed, but renewed his suit, on our return in the afternoon, with such warmth of solicitation, as to cause an evident alteration in the sentiments of the lady.

To heighten the good humour which pervaded both parties, we began to play and romp with them. Feats of bodily strength were tried, and their inferiority was glaring. One of our party lifted with ease two of them from the ground, in spite of their efforts to prevent him; whereas in return, no one of them could move him: they called him *Mùr-ree Mùl-la* (a large strong man). Compared with our English labourers, their muscular power would appear very feeble and inadequate.

Before we parted, Baneelon informed us, that his countrymen had lately been plundered of fish-gigs, spears, a sword, and many other articles, by some of our people; and expressed a wish that they should be restored, promising, that if they were, the govervor's dirk should be produced, and returned to us to-morrow, if we would meet him here.

September 1790. Accordingly on the following day we rowed to the spot, carrying with us the stolen property. We found here several natives, but not Baneelon. We asked for him, and were told that he was gone down the harbour with Barangaroo to fish. Although disappointed at his breach of promise, we went on shore, and mingled without distrust among those we found, acquainting them that we had brought with us the articles of which they had been plundered. On hearing this account, they expressed great joy, and Imeerawanyee darting forward, claimed the sword. It was given to him, and he had no sooner grasped it, than he hastened to convince his mistress, that his prowess in war, was not inferior to his skill in courtship. Singling out a yellow gum-tree for the foe, he attacked it with great fierceness, calling to us to look on, and accompanying his onset with all the gestures and vociferation which they use in battle. Having conquered his enemy, he laid aside his fighting face, and joined us with a countenance which carried in it every mark of youth and good nature.

Whether Abaroo's coyness, and preference of another, had displeased him, or it was owing to natural fickleness, he paid

K

her no farther attention, but seemed more delighted with us. He had no beard: but was highly gratified in being combed and having his hair clipped.

All the stolen property being brought on shore, an old man came up, and claimed one of the fish-gigs, singling it from the bundle, and taking only his own; and this honesty, within the circle of their society, seemed to characterize them all.

September, 1790. During this time, it was observed, that one of the Indians, instead of mixing with the rest, stood aloof, in a musing posture, contemplating what passed. When we offered to approach him, he shunned us not, and willingly shook hands with all who chose to do so. He seemed to be between 30 and 40 years old, was jolly, and had a thoughtful countenance, much marked by the small-pox. He wore a string of bits of dried reed, round his neck, which I asked him to exchange for a black stock. He smiled at the proposal, but made no offer of what I wanted; which our young friend, Imeerawanyee, observing, flew to him, and taking off the necklace, directly fixed it about my neck. I feared he would be enraged; but he bore it with serenity, and suffered a gentleman present to fasten his black stock upon him, with which he appeared to be pleased; to increase his satisfaction, some other trifle was given to him.

Having remained here an hour, we went in quest of Baneelon, agreeably to the directions which his companions pointed out. We found him and Barangaroo shivering over a few lighted sticks, by which they were dressing small fish, and their canoe hauled up on the beach near them. On first seeing the boat, they ran into the woods; but on being called by name, they came back, and consented to our landing. We carried on shore with us the remaining part of the fish-gigs and spears which had been stolen, and restored them to Baneelon. Among other things, was a net full of fishing lines and other tackle, which Barangaroo said was her property, and immediately on receiving it, she slung it around her neck.

Baneelon inquired, with solicitude, about the state of the governor's wound ; but he made no offer of restoring the dirk ; and when he was asked for it, he pretended to know nothing of it, changing the conversation with great art, and asking for wine, which was given to him.

At parting, we pressed him to appoint a day on which he should come to Sydney, assuring him, that he would be well received, and kindly treated. Doubtful, however, of being permitted to return, he evaded our request, and declared, that the governor must first come and see him, which we promised should be done.

The governor did not hesitate to execute the engagement which we had contracted for him. But Baneelon still resisted coming among us, and matters continued in this fluctuating state until the 8th of October, when a fire, which they had agreed to light as a signal for us to visit them, was observed ; the eager desire, by which we were stimulated to carry our point of effecting an intercourse, has appeared : various parties accordingly set out to meet them, provided with different articles, which we thought would prove acceptable to them. We found assembled, Baneelon, Barangaroo, and another young woman, and six men, all of whom received us with welcome, except the grave looking gentleman beforementioned, who stood aloof in his former musing posture. When they saw that we had brought hatchets, and other articles with us, they produced spears, fish-gigs, and lines, for the purpose of barter*, which immediately commenced, to the satisfaction of

---

* It had long been our wish to establish a commerce of this sort. It is a painful consideration, that every previous addition to the cabinet of the virtuosi, from this country, had wrung a tear from the plundered Indian.

both parties. I had brought with me an old blunted spear, which wanted repair. An Indian immediately undertook to perform the task, and carrying it to a fire, tore with his teeth a piece of bone from a fish-gig, which he fastened on the spear with yellow gum, rendered flexible by heat.

October, 1790. Many of them now consented to be shaved by a barber whom we had purposely brought over. As I thought he who could perform an operation of such importance, must be deemed by them an eminent personage, I bade him ask one of them for a fine barbed spear which he held in his hand; but all the barber's eloquence was wasted on the Indian, who plainly gave him to understand, that he meant not to part with his spear, without receiving an equivalent. Unfortunately, his price was a hatchet, and the only one which I had brought with me, was already disposed of to the man who had pointed my spear. In vain did I tempt him with a knife, a handkerchief, and a hat; nothing but a hatchet seemed to be re-regarded. *Bùlla Mògo Parrabugò* (two hatchets to-morrow) I repeatedly cried; but having probably experienced our insincerity, he rejected the proposal with disdain. Finding him inflexible, and longing to possess the spear, I told him at length that I would go to Sydney and fetch what he required. This seemed to satisfy, and he accompanied me to my boat, in which I went away, and as quickly as possible, procured what was necessary to conclude the bargain. On my return, I was surprised to see all our boats rowing towards home, and with them a canoe, in which sat two Indians paddling. I pulled to them, and found that Baneelon, and another Indian, were in one of the boats; and that the whole formed a party going over to visit the governor. I now learned, that during my absence, the governor had passed in a boat, on his return from Rose-hill, near the place where they were standing; and that finding he would not come to them, although they had called to him to do so, they had at once determined to venture themselves unreservedly among us. One of the men in the canoe, was the person to whom I was to give the hatchet I had been to fetch ; and directly as he saw me, he held up his spear, and the exchange took place, with which, and perhaps to reward me for the trouble I had taken, he was so delighted, that he presented me with a throwing-stick *gratis.*

October, 1790. Not seeing Barangaroo of the party, I asked for her, and was informed, that she had violently opposed Baneelon's departure. When she found persuasion vain, she had recourse to tears, scolding, and threats, stamping the ground, and tearing her hair. But Baneelon continuing determined; she snatched up in her rage one of his fish-gigs, and dashed it with such fury on the rocks, that it broke. To quiet her apprehensions, on the score of her husband's safety, Mr. Johnson, attended by Abaroo, agreed to remain as a hostage until Baneelon should return.

We landed our four friends opposite the hospital, and set out for the governor's house. On hearing of their arrival, such numbers flocked to view them, that we were apprehensive, the croud of persons would alarm them ; but they had left their fears behind, and marched on with boldness and unconcern. When we reached the governor's house, Baneelon expressed honest joy to see his old friend, and appeared pleased to find that he had recovered of his wound. The governor asked for Wileemarin, and they said he was at Broken Bay Some bread and beef were distributed among them ; but unluckily no fish was to be procured, which we were sorry for, as a promise of it had been one of the leading temptations by which they had been allured over. A hatchet a-piece was, however, given to them, and a couple of petticoats and some fishing tackle sent for Barangaroo, and the other woman.

The ceremony of introduction being finished, Baneelon seemed

to consider himself quite at home, running from room to room with
his companions, and introducing them to his old friends, the do-
mestics, in the most familiar manner. Among these last, he particularly distinguished the governor's orderly serjeant, whom he
kissed with great affection, and a woman who attended in the
kitchen; but the gamekeeper, M'Entire,* he continued to hold
in abhorrence, and would not suffer his approach.

October, 1790. Nor was his importance to his countrymen less
conspicuous in other respects: he undertook to explain the use and
nature of those things which were new to them. Some of his explanations were whimsical enough.—Seeing, for instance, a pair of
snuffers, he told them that they were " *Nuffer* † *for candle*," which
the others not comprehending, he opened the snuffers, and holding
up the fore-finger of his left hand, to represent a candle, made the
motion of snuffing it. Finding, that even this sagacious interpre-
tation failed, he threw down the snuffers in a rage, and reproaching their stupidity, walked away.

It was observed, that a soft gentle tone of voice, which we had
taught him to use, was forgotten, and his native vociferation returned in full force. But the tenderness which (like Arabanoo)
he had always manifested to children, he still retained; as appeared
by his behaviour to those who were presented to him.

October, 1790. The first wish they expressed to return, was
complied with, in order to banish all appearance of constraint; the
party who had conducted them to Sydney returning with them.
When we reached the opposite shore, we found Abaroo and the

* Look at the account of the governor being wounded, when his detestation of this man
burst forth.

† The S is a letter which they cannot pronounce, having no sound in their language similar to it. When bidden to pronounce sun, they always say *tun*; salt, *talt*; and so of all
words wherein it occurs.

other woman fishing in a canoe, and Mr. Johnson and Barangaroo sitting at the fire, the latter employed in manufacturing fish-hooks. At a little distance, on an adjoining eminence, sat an Indian, with his spear in his hand, as if centinel over the hostages, for the security of his countrymen's return. During our absence, Barangaroo had never ceased whining, and reproaching her husband; now that he was returned, she met him with unconcern, and seemed intent on her work only: but this state of repose did not long continue: Baneelon eyeing the broken fish-gig, cast at her a look of savage fury, and began to interrogate her; and it seemed more than probable, that the remaining part would be demolished about her head, had we not interposed to pacify him. Nor would we quit the place until his forgiveness was complete, and his good humour restored. No sooner, however, did she find her husband's rage subsided, than her hour of triumph commenced. The alarm and trepidation she had manifested, disappeared: elated at his condescension, and emboldened by our presence, and the finery in which we had decked her, she in turn assumed a haughty demeanour, refused to answer his caresses, and viewed him with a reproaching eye.—Although long absence from female society had somewhat blunted our recollection, the conduct of Barangaroo did not appear quite novel to us; nor was our surprise very violent at finding that it succeeded in subduing Baneelon, who, when we parted, seemed anxious only to please her.

Thus ended a day, the events of which served to complete, what an unhappy accident had begun. From this time our intercourse with the natives, though partially interrupted, was never broken off. We gradually continued, henceforth, to gain knowledge of their customs and policy:—the only knowledge which can lead to a just estimate of national character.

CHAPTER X.

The arrival of the Supply from BATAVIA:—*The State of the Colony in November,* 1790.

J OY sparkled in every countenance to see our old friend the Supply (I hope no reader will be so captious as to quarrel with the phrase) enter the harbour from Batavia, on the 19th of October. We had witnessed her departure with tears:—we hailed her return with transport.

Captain Ball was rather more than six months in making this voyage; and is the first person who ever circumnavigated the continent of New Holland. On his passage to Batavia, he had discovered several islands, which he gave names to ; and after fighting his way against adverse elements, and through unexplored dangers, safely reached his destined port. He had well stored his little bark with every necessary and conveniency, which he judged we should first want ; leaving a cargo of rice and salt provisions to be brought on by a Dutch snow, which he had hired and freighted for the use of the settlement. While at Batavia, the Supply had lost many of her people by sickness, and left several others in the general hospital at that place

As the arrival of the Supply naturally leads the attention from other subjects to the state of the colony, I shall here take a review of it, by transcribing a statement, drawn from actual observation, soon after, exactly as I find it written in my journal.

November, 1790. ' Cultivation, on a public scale, has for some
' time past been given up here, (Sydney) the crop of last year
' being so miserable, as to deter from farther experiment; in con-
' sequence of which, the government-farm is abandoned, and the
' people who were fixed on it, have been removed. Necessary
' public buildings advance fast ; an excellent storehouse, of large
' dimensions, built of bricks, and covered with tiles, is just com-
' pleted ; and another planned, which will shortly be begun.
' Other buildings, among which I heard the governor mention an
' hospital, and permanent barracks for the troops, may also be ex-
' pected to arise soon. Works of this nature are more expedi-
' tiously performed than heretofore, owing, I apprehend, to the
' superintendants lately arrived, who are placed over the convicts,
' and compel them to labour. The first difficulties of a new coun-
' try being subdued, may also contribute to this comparative
' facility.

' Vegetables are scarce, although the summer is so far advanced,
' owing to want of rain. I do not think that all the showers of the
' last four months put together, would make 24 hours rain. Our
' farms, what with this, and a poor soil, are in wretched condition.
' My winter crop of potatoes, which I planted in days of despair,
' (March and April last) turned out very badly, when I dug them
' about two months back. Wheat returned so poorly last harvest,
' that very little, besides Indian corn, has been sown this year. The
' governor's wound is quite healed, and he feels no inconveniency
' whatever from it. With the natives we are hand and glove. They
' throng the camp every day, and sometimes by their clamour and
' importunity for bread and meat (of which they now all eat gree-
' dily) are become very troublesome. God knows, we have little

L

' enough for ourselves! Full allowance (if eight pounds of flour, and
' either seven pounds of beef, or four pounds of pork, served al-
' ternately, per week, without either pease, oatmeal, spirits, butter,
' or cheese, can be called so) is yet kept up; but if the Dutch snow
' does not arrive soon it must be shortened, as the casks in the
' storehouse, I observed yesterday, are woefully decreased.

' The convicts continue to behave pretty well; three only have
' been hanged since the arrival of the last fleet, in the latter end
' of June, all of whom were new comers. The number of convicts
' here diminishes every day; our principal efforts being wisely made
' at Rose Hill, where the land is unquestionably better than about
' this place. Except building, sawing, and brick-making, nothing
' of consequence is now carried on here. The account which I re-
' ceived a few days ago from the brick-makers of their labours,
' was as follows: Wheeler (one of the master brick-makers) with
' two tile stools, and one brick stool, was tasked to make and
' burn ready for use 30000 tiles and bricks per month; he had
' 21 hands to assist him, who performed every thing; cut wood,
' dug clay, &c. This continued (during the days of distress ex-
' cepted, when they did what they could) until June last. From
' June, with one brick and two tile stools he has been tasked to
' make 40000 bricks and tiles monthly, (as many of each sort as
' may be) having 22 men and two boys to assist him, on the same
' terms of procuring materials as before. They fetch the clay of
' which tiles are made, two hundred yards; that for bricks is close
' at hand.—He says that the bricks are such as would be called in
' England, moderately good; and he judges they would have
' fetched about 24s. per thousand, at Kingston-upon-Thames,
' (where he resided) in the year 1784: their greatest fault is being
' too brittle. The tiles he thinks not so good as those made
' about London: the stuff has a rotten quality, and besides wants

' the advantage of being ground, in lieu of which they tread
' it.

' November, 1790. King (another master bricklayer) last year,
' with the assistance of 16 men and two boys, made 11000 thou-
' sand bricks weekly, with two stools. During short allowance
' did what he could : resumed his old task when put again on full
' allowance ; and had his number of assistants augmented to 20
' men and two boys, on account of the increased distance of car-
' rying wood for the kilns. He worked at Hammersmith, for
' Mr. Scot, of that place. He thinks the bricks made here as good
' as those made near London ; and says that in the year 1784, they
' would have sold for a guinea per thousand ; and to have picked
' the kiln at thirty shillings.

Such is my Sydney detail, dated on the 12th of November,
1790 : Four days after I went to Rose Hill, and wrote there the
subjoined remarks.

' November 16th. Got to Rose Hill in the evening : Next morn-
' ing walked round the whole of the cleared and cultivated land,
' with the Rev. Mr. Johnson, who is the best farmer in the coun-
' try. Edward Dod, one of the governor's household, who con-
' ducts every thing here in the agricultural line, accompanied us
' part of the way, and afforded all the information he could. He
' estimates the quantity of cleared and cultivated land at 200 acres.
' Of these 55 are in wheat, barley, and a little oats, 30 in maize,
' and the remainder is either just cleared of wood, or is occupied by
' buildings, gardens, &c. Four inclosures of 20 acres each, are
' planned for the reception of cattle, which may arrive in the colo-
' ny, and two of these are already fenced in. In the centre of them
' is to be erected a house, for a person who will be fixed upon to
' take care of the cattle. All these inclosures are supplied with
' water ; and only a part of the trees which grew in them being

' cut down, gives to them a very park-like and beautiful appear-
' ance.

Our survey commenced on the north side of the river. : Dod says
' he expects this year's crop of wheat and barley from the 55 acres
' to yield full 400 bushels. Appearances hitherto hardly indicate
' so much. He says he finds the beginning of May the best time
' to sow barley ; * but that it may continue to be sown until Au-
' gust : that sown in May is reaped in December ; that of August
' in January. He sowed his wheat, part in June and part in July.
' He thinks June the best time ; and says that he invariably finds
' that which is deepest sown, grows strongest and best : even as
' deep as three inches he has put it in, and found it to answer. The
' wheat sown in June is now turning yellow ; that of July is more
' backward. He has used only the broad-cast husbandry, and sowed
' two bushels per acre. The plough has never yet been tried here ; all
' the ground is hoed, and (as Dod confesses) very incompetently
' turned up. Each convict labourer was obliged to hoe sixteen rods
' a day, so that in some places the earth was but just scratched over.
' The ground was left open for some months, to receive benefit from
' the sun and air ; and on that newly cleared the trees were burnt,
' and the ashes dug in. I do not find that a succession of crops has
' yet been attempted, surely it would help to meliorate and im-
' prove the soil. Dod recommends strongly the culture of potatoes,
' on a large scale, and says that were they planted, even as late as
' January, they would answer ; but this I doubt. He is more than
' ever of opinion that without a large supply of cattle nothing
' can be done. They have not at this time either horse, cow, or
' sheep here. I asked him how the stock they had was coming
' on. The fowls he said multiplied exceedingly ; but the hogs

---

* The best crop of barley ever produced in New South Wales, was sown by a private individual, in February 1790, and reaped in the following October.

neither thrived, or increased in number, for want of food. He
pointed out to us his best wheat, which looks tolerable, and may
perhaps yield 13 or 14 bushels per acre.*   Next came the oats
which are in ear, though not more than six inches high: they
will not return as much seed as was sown.   The barley, except
one patch in a corner of a field, little better than the oats. Crossed the river and inspected the south side.   Found the little patch
of wheat at the bottom of the cresent very bad : proceeded and
examined the large field on the ascent to the westward : here are
about 25 acres of wheat, which from its appearance we guessed
would produce perhaps seven bushels an acre.   The next patch
to this is in maize, which looks not unpromising ; some of
the stems are stout, and beginning to throw out large broad leaves,
the surest sign of vigour. The view from the top of the wheat
field takes in, except a narrow slip, the whole of the cleared land
at Rose Hill.   From not having before seen an opening of such
extent for the last three years, this struck us as grand and capacious.   The beautiful diversity of the ground (gentle hill and
dale) would certainly be reckoned pretty in any country.   Continued our walk, and crossed the old field, which is intended to
form part of the main street of the projected town.   The wheat
in this field is rather better, but not much, than in the large field
before mentioned.   The next field is maize, inferior to what we

---

* As all the trees on our cleared ground were cut down, and not grubbed up, the roots and
stumps remain ; on which account a tenth part of surface in every acre must be deducted.
This is slovenly husbandry ; but in a country where immediate subsistence is wanted, it is
perhaps necessary.   None of these stumps, when I left Port Jackson, shewed any symptoms
of decay, though some of the trees had been cut down four years.   To the different qualities of the wood of Norfolk Island and New South Wales, perhaps the difference of soil
may in some measure be traced.   That of Norfolk Island is light and porous : it rots and turns
into mould in two years. Besides its hardness that of Port Jackson abounds with red corro-
sive gum, which contributes its share of mischief.

' have seen, but not despicable: an acre of maize, at the bottom of
' the marine garden, is equal in luxuriancy of promise to any I ever
' saw in any country.

    ' The main street of the new town is already begun. It is to
' be a mile long, and of such breadth as will make Pall-Mall and
' Portland-Place " hide their diminished heads." ' It contains at
' present 32 houses completed, of 24 feet by 12 each, on a ground
' floor only, built of wattles plaistered with clay, and thatched.
' Each house is divided into two rooms, in one of which is a fire
' place and a brick chimney. These houses are designed for men
' only; and ten is the number of inhabitants allotted to each; but
' some of them now contain 12 or 14, for want of better ac-
' commodation. More are building; in a cross street stand nine
' houses for unmarried women: and exclusive of all these are se-
' veral small huts where convict families of good character are al-
' lowed to reside. Of public buildings, besides the old wooden bar-
' rack and store, there is a house of lath and plaister, 44 feet long
' by 16 wide, for the governor, on a ground floor only, with ex-
' cellent out-houses and appurtenances attached to it. A new
' brick store-house, covered with tiles, 100 feet long by 24 wide,
' is nearly completed, and a house for the store-keeper. The first
' stone of a barrack, 100 feet long by 24 wide, to which are inten-
' ded to be added wings for the officers, was laid to-day. The si-
' tuation of the barrack is judicious, being close to the store-house,
' and within a hundred and fifty yards of the wharf, where all boats
' from Sydney unload. To what I have already enumerated, must
' be added an excellent barn, a granary, an inclosed yard to rear
' stock in, a commodious blacksmith's shop, and a most wretched
' hospital, totally destitute of every conveniency. Luckily for the
' gentleman who superintends this hospital, and still more luckily
' for those who are doomed in case of sickness to enter it, the air

' of Rose Hill has hitherto been generally healthy. A tendency to
' produce slight inflammatory disorders, from the rapid changes * of
' the temperature of the air, is most to be dreaded.

' The hours of labour for the convicts are the same here as at
' Sydney. On Saturdays after ten o'clock in the morning they are
' allowed to work in their own gardens: these gardens are at
' present, from the long drought, and other causes, in a most deplo-
' rable state : potatoes, I think, thrive better than any other vege-
' table in them. For the public conveniency a baker is established
' here in a good bakehouse, who exchanges with every person
' bread for flour, on stipulated terms ; but no compulsion exists
' for any one to take his bread ; it is left entirely to every body's
' own option to consume his flour as he pleases. Divine service is
' performed here, morning and afternoon, one Sunday in every
' month, when all the convicts are obliged to attend church, under
' penalty of having a part of their allowance of provisions stopped,
' which is done by the chaplain, who is a justice of the peace.

' For the punishment of offenders, where a criminal court is
' not judged necessary, two, or more justices, occasionally assemble,
' and order the infliction of slight corporal punishment, or short
' confinement in a strong room, built for this purpose. The mi-
' litary present here consists of two subalterns, two serjeants, three
' corporals, a drummer, and 21 privates. These have been occa-
' sionally augmented and reduced, as circumstances have been
' thought to render it necessary.

' Brick-kilns are now erected here, and bricks manufactured by
' a convict of the name of Becket, who came out in the last fleet,
' and has 52 people to work under him. He makes 25,000 bricks

* In the close of the year 1788, when this settlement was established, the thermometer
has been known to stand at 50° a little before sun-rise, and between one and two o'clock in
the afternoon at above 100°.

‘ weekly. He says that they are very good, and would sell at Bir-
‘ mingham, where he worked about eighteen months ago, at more
‘ than 30 s. per thousand.

‘ Nothing farther of public nature remaining to examine, I
‘ next visited a humble adventurer, who is trying his fortune here.
‘ James Ruse, convict, was cast for seven years at Bodmin assizes,
‘ in August 1782 ; he lay five years in prison and on board the
‘ Dunkirk hulk at Plymouth, and then was sent to this coun-
‘ try. When his term of punishment expired, in August 1789,
‘ he claimed his freedom, and was permitted by the governor,
‘ on promising to settle in the country, to take in December
‘ following, an uncleaned piece of ground, with an assurance that
‘ if he would cultivate it, it should not be taken from him. Some
‘ assistance was given him, to fell the timber, and he accordingly
‘ began. His present account to me was as follows. “I was bred
‘ a husbandman, near Launcester in Cornwall. I cleared my land
‘ as well as I could, with the help afforded me. The exact limit of
‘ what ground I am to have, I do not yet know ; but a certain di-
“ rection has been pointed out to me, in which I may proceed as
“ fast as I can cultivate. I have now an acre and a half in bearded
“ wheat, half an acre in maize, and a small kitchen garden. On my
“ wheat land I sowed three bushels of seed, the produce of this
“ country, broad cast. I expect to reap about 12 or 13 bushels.—
“ I know nothing of the cultivation of maize, and cannot therefore
“ guess so well at what I am likely to gather. I sowed part of
“ my wheat in May, and part in June.—That sown in May has
“ thriven best. My maize I planted in the latter end of August,
“ and the beginning of September. My land I prepared thus: hav-
“ ing burnt the fallen timber off the ground, I dug in the ashes,
“ and then hoed it up, never doing more than eight, or perhaps
“ nine, rods in a day, by which means, it was not like the govern-

" ment-farm, just scratched over, but properly done; then I clod-
" moulded it, and dug in the grass and weeds:—this I think almost
" equal to ploughing. I then let it lie as long as I could, exposed to
" air and sun; and just before I sowed my seed, turned it all up
" afresh.—When I shall have reaped my crop, I purpose to hoe it
" again, and harrow it fine, and then sow it with turnip-seed,
" which will mellow and prepare it for next year.—My straw, I
" mean to bury in pits, and throw in with it every thing which I
" think will rot and turn to manure. I have no person to help
" me, at present, but my wife, whom I married in this country :
" she is industrious. The governor, for some time, gave me the
" help of a convict man, but he is taken away. Both my wife
" and myself receive our provisions regularly at the store, like all
" other people. My opinion of the soil of my farm, is, that it is
" middling, neither good or bad. I will be bound to make it do
" with the aid of manure, but without cattle it will fail.—The
" greatest check upon me is, the dishonesty of the convicts, who,
" in spite of all my vigilance, rob me almost every night."

November, 1790. The annexed return, will shew the number of persons of all descriptions at Rose Hill, at this period —On the morning of the 17th, I went down to Sydney.

Here terminates the transcription of my diary.—It were vain to suppose, that it can prove either agreeable or interesting to a majority of readers: but as this work is intended not only for amusement, but information, I considered it right to present this detail unaltered, either in its style or arrangement.

M

A return of the number of persons employed at Rose Hill, November 16th, 1790.

How employed.	Troops.	Civil department.	Troops.		Convicts.		
			Wives.	Children.	Men.	Women.	Children.
Storekeeper – –	–	1					
Surgeon – – –	–	1					
Carpenters – –	–	–	–	–	24		
Blacksmiths –	–	–	–	–	5		
Master Bricklayer –	–	–	–	–	1		
Bricklayers – –	–	–	–	–	28		
Master Brickmaker –	–	–	–	–	1		
Brickmakers –	–	–	–	–	52		
Labourers – –	–	–	–	–	326*		
Assistants to the provision store – – –	–	–	–	–	4		
Assistants to the hospital –	–	–	–	–	3		
Officers' servants – –	–	–	–	–	6		
Making clothing – –	–	–	–	–	–	50	
Superintendants – –	–	4	–	–			
Total number of persons 552	29	6	1	3	450	50	13

* Of these labourers, 16 are sawyers. The rest are variously employed in clearing fresh land; in dragging brick and timber carts; and a great number in making a road of a mile long, through the main street, to the governor's house.

CHAPTER XI.

Farther Transactions of the Colony in November, 1790.

DURING the intervals of duty, our greatest source of entertainment now lay in cultivating the acquaintance of our new friends, the natives. Ever liberal of communication, no difficulty, but of understanding each other, subsisted between us. Inexplicable contradictions arose to bewilder our researches, which no ingenuity could unravel, and no credulity reconcile.

Baneelon, from being accustomed to our manners, and understanding a little English, was the person through whom we wished to prosecute inquiry: but he had lately become a man of so much dignity and consequence, that it was not always easy to obtain his company. Clothes had been given to him at various times; but he did not always condescend to wear them: one day he would appear in them; and the next day he was to be seen carrying them in a net, slung around his neck. Farther to please him, a brick house, of 12 feet square, was built for his use, and for that of such of his countrymen as might chuse to reside in it, on a point of land fixed upon by himself. A shield, double cased with tin, to ward off the spears of his enemies, was also presented to him, by the governor.

November, 1790. Elated by these marks of favour, and sensible that his importance with his countrymen arose, in proportion to our patronage of him, he warmly attached himself to our society.

But the gratitude of a savage is ever a precarious tenure: that of
Baneelon was fated to suffer suspension, and had well nigh been
obliterated by the following singular circumstance.

One day, the natives were observed to assemble in more than an
ordinary number, at their house on the point, and to be full of
bustle and agitation, repeatedly calling on the name of Baneelon,
and that of *Dee-in* (a woman). Between twelve and one o'clock
Baneelon, unattended, came to the governor, at his house, and told
him that he was going to put to death a woman immediately,
whom he had brought from Botany Bay. Having communicated
his intention, he was preparing to go away, seeming not to wish
that the governor should be present at the performance of the ceremony. But his excellency was so struck with the fierce gestures,
and wild demeanour of the other, who held in his hand one of our
hatchets, and frequently tried the sharpness of it, that he determined to accompany him, taking with him Mr. Collins, and his
orderly serjeant. On the road, Baneelon continued to talk wildly
and incoherently of what he would do, and manifested such extravagant marks of fury and revenge, that his hatchet was taken
away from him, and a walking-stick substituted for it. When they
reached the house, they found several natives, of both sexes, lying
promiscuously before the fire, and among them, a young woman,
not more than 16 years old, who at sight of Baneelon, started, and
raised herself half up. He no sooner saw her, than snatching a
sword of the country, he ran at her, and gave her two severe
wounds on the head, and one on the shoulder, before interference
in behalf of the poor wretch could be made. Our people now
rushed in, and seized him; but the other Indians continued quiet
spectators of what was passing, either awed by Baneelon's superiority, or deeming it a common case, unworthy of notice and in-
terposition.—In vain did the governor by turns soothe and

threaten him ;—in vain did the serjeant point his musquet at him; he seemed dead to every passion but revenge; forgot his affection to his old friends; and, instead of complying with the request they made, furiously brandished his sword at the governor, and called aloud for his hatchet to dispatch the unhappy victim of his barbarity. Matters now wore a serious aspect: the other Indians appeared under the controul of Baneelon, and had begun to arm, and prepare their spears, as if determined to support him in his violence.

November, 1790. Farther delay might have been attended with danger: the Supply was therefore immediately hailed, and an armed boat ordered to be sent on shore. Luckily, those on board the ship had already observed the commotion, and a boat was ready, into which captain Ball, with several of his people stepped, armed with musquets, and put off. It was reasonable to believe, that so powerful a reinforcement would restore tranquillity; but Baneelon stood unintimidated at disparity of numbers, and boldly demanded his prisoner, whose life, he told the governor, he was determined to sacrifice, and afterwards to cut off her head. Every one was eager to know what could be the cause of such inveterate inhumanity. Undaunted, he replied, that her father was his enemy, from whom he had received the wound in his forehead, beforementioned ; and that when he was down in battle, and under the lance of his antagonist, this woman had contributed to assail him. " She is now," added he, " my property: I have ravished " her by force from her tribe: and I will part with her to no per- " son whatever, until my vengeance shall be glutted."

Farther remonstrance would have been wasted ; his excellency therefore ordered the woman to be taken to the hospital, in order that her wounds might be dressed. While this was doing, one of the natives, a young man, named Bol-a-dèr-ee, came up and supplicated to be taken into the boat also, saying that he was her husband, which she confirmed, and begged that he might be admitted. He was a fine well grown lad, of 19 or 20 years old, and was one of the persons who had been in the house in the scene just described, which he had in no wise endeavoured to prevent ; or to afford assistance to the poor creature who had a right to his protection.

All our people now quitted the place, leaving the exasperated Baneelon and his associates to meditate farther schemes of vengeance. Before they parted he gave them, however, to understand, that he would follow the object of his resentment to the hospital, and kill her there : a threat which the governor assured him if he offered to carry into execution he should be immediately shot. Even this menace he treated with disdain.

To place the refugees in security, a centinel was ordered to take post at the door of the house, in which they were lodged. Nevertheless they attempted to get away in the night, either from fear that we were not able to protect them, or some apprehension of being restrained from future liberty. When questioned where they proposed to find shelter, they said they would go to the Cameragal tribe, with whom they should be safe. On the following morning Imeerawanyee * joined them, and expressed strong fears of Baneelon's resentment. Soon after a party of natives, known to consist of Baneelon's chosen friends, with a man of the name of Bì-gon,

* This good-tempered lively lad, was become a great favourite with us, and almost constantly lived at the governor's house. He had clothes made up for him ; and to amuse his mind, he was taught to wait at table. One day a lady, Mrs. M‘Arthur, wife of an officer of the garrison, dined there, as did Nanbaree. This latter, anxious that his countryman should appear to advantage in his new office, gave him many instructions, strictly charging him, among other things, to take away the lady's plate, whenever she should cross her knife and fork, and to give her a clean one. This Imeerawanyee executed, not only to Mrs. M‘Arthur, but to several of the other guests. At last Nanbaree crossed his knife and fork with great gravity, casting a glance at the other, who looked for a moment with cool indifference at what

at their head, boldly entered the hospital garden, and tried to carry off all three by force. They were driven back and threatned ;
to which their leader only replied by contemptuous insolence.

Baneelon finding he could not succeed, withdrew himself for two
days. At length he made his appearance, attended only by his wife.
Unmindful of what had so recently happened, he marched singly
up to the governor's house, and on being refused admittance, though
unarmed, attempted to force the centinel. The soldier spared him ;
but the guard was instantly sent for, and drawn up in front of
the house ; not that their co-operation was necessary, but that their
appearance might terrify. His ardour now cooled, and he seemed
willing, by submission, to atone for his misconduct. His intrepid dis-
regard of personal risque, nay of life, could not however, but gain
admiration ; though it led us to predict, that this Baneelon, whom
imagination had fondly pictured, like a second Omai, the gaze of a
court, and the scrutiny of the curious, would perish untimely, the
victim of his own temerity.

To encourage his present disposition of mind : and to try if feelings of compassion towards an enemy, could be exerted by an Indian
warrior, the governor ordered him to be taken to the hospital, that
he might see the victim of his ferocity. He complied in sullen silence. When about to enter the room in which she lay, he appeared to have a momentary struggle with himself, which ended his resentment. He spoke to her with kindness ; and professed sorrow for
what he had done ; and promised her future protection. Barangaroo, who had accompanied him, now took the alarm : and as

he had done, and then turned his head another way. Stung at this supercilious treatment,
he called in rage, to know why he was not attended to, as well as the rest of the company.
But Imeerawanyee only laughed ; nor could all the anger and reproaches of the other prevail
upon him to do that for one of his countrymen, which he cheerfully continued to perform to
every other person.

in shunning one extreme, we are ever likely to rush into another, she thought him perhaps too courteous and tender. Accordingly she began to revile them both with great bitterness; threw stones at the girl; and attempted to beat her with a club.

November, 1790. Here terminated this curious history, which I leave to the reader's speculation. Whether human sacrifices of prisoners be common among them is a point, which all our future inquiry never completely determined. It is certain that no second instance of this sort was ever witnessed by us.

CHAPTER XII.

Transactions of the Colony in Part of December, 1790.

ON the 9th of the month, a serjeant of marines, with three con-victs, among whom was M'Entire, the governor's gamekeeper (the person of whom Baneelon had, on former occasions, shewn so much dread and hatred) went out on a shooting party. Having passed the north arm of Botany Bay, they proceeded to a hut formed of boughs, which had been lately erected on this peninsula, for the accommodation of sportsmen who wished to continue by night in the woods : for, as the kanguroos in the day-time, chiefly keep in the cover, it is customary on these parties to sleep until near sunset, and watch for the game during the night, and in the early part of the morning. Accordingly, having lighted a fire, they lay down, without distrust or suspicion.

December, 1790. About one o'clock, the serjeant was awakened by a rustling noise in the bushes near him, and supposing it to proceed from a kanguroo, called to his comrades, who instantly jumped up. On looking about more narrowly, they saw two na-tives, with spears in their hands, creeping towards them, and three others a little farther behind. As this naturally created alarm, M'Entire said, 'don't be afraid, I know them,' and imme-diately laying down his gun, stepped forward, and spoke to them in their own language. The Indians, finding they were discovered, kept slowly retreating, and M'Entire accompanied them about a hundred yards, talking familiarly all the while. One of them now

N

jumped on a fallen tree, and without giving the least warning of his intention, launched his spear at M'Entire, and lodged it in his left side. The person who committed this wanton act, was described as a young man, with a speck, or blemish, on his left eye; that he had been lately among us, was evident from his being newly shaved.

The wounded man immediately drew back, and joining his party, cried, ' I am a dead man.' While one broke off the end of the spear, the other two set out with their guns in pursuit of the natives; but their swiftness of foot, soon convinced our people of the impossibility of reaching them. It was now determined to attempt to carry M'Entire home, as his death was apprehended to be near, and he expressed a longing desire not to be left to expire in the woods. Being an uncommonly robust muscular man, notwithstanding a great effusion of blood, he was able, with the assistance of his comrades, to creep slowly along, and reached Sydney about two o'clock the next morning On the wound being examined by the surgeons, it was pronounced mortal. The poor wretch now began to utter the most dreadful exclamations, and to accuse himself of the commission of crimes of the deepest dye; accompanied with such expressions of his despair of God's mercy, as are too terrible to repeat.

In the course of the day, Colbee, and several more natives came in, and were taken to the bed where the wounded man lay. Their behaviour indicated, that they had already heard of the accident, as they repeated twice or thrice the name of the murderer Pim-el-wi, saying, that he lived at Botany Bay. To gain knowledge of their treatment of similar wounds, one of the surgeons made signs of extracting the spear; but this they violently opposed, and said, if it were done, death would instantly follow.

On the 12th, the extraction of the spear was, however, judged practicable, and was accordingly performed. That part of it which had penetrated the body, measured seven inches and a half long, having on it a wooden barb, and several smaller ones of stone, fastened on with yellow gum, most of which, owing to the force necessary in extraction, were torn off and lodged in the patient. The spear had passed between two ribs, and had wounded the left lobe of the lungs. He lingered * until the 20th of January, and then expired. On opening the corpse, it was found that the left lung had perished from suppuration, its remains adhering to the ribs. Some pieces of stone, which had dropped from the spear, were seen, but no barb of wood.

December, 1790. The governor was at Rose-hill when this accident happened. On the day after he returned to Sydney, the following order was issued :—" Several tribes of the natives still con-
" tinuing to throw spears at any man they meet unarmed, by
" which several have been killed, or dangerously wounded :—the
" governor, in order to deter the natives from such practices in fu-
" ture, has ordered out a party to search for the man who wounded
" the convict M'Entire, in so dangerous a manner on Friday last,
" though no offence was offered on his part, in order to make a
" signal example of that tribe. At the same time, the governor
" strictly forbids, under penalty of the severest punishment, any
" soldier, or other person, not expressly ordered out for that pur-
" pose, ever to fire on any native except in his own defence ; or to
" molest him in any shape, or to bring away any spears, or other

---

* From the aversion uniformly shewn by all the natives to this unhappy man, he had long been suspected by us of having in his excursions, shot and injured them. To gain information on this head from him, the moment of contrition was seized. On being questioned with great seriousness, he, however, declared that he had never fired but once on a native, and then had not killed, but severely wounded him, and this in his own defence. Notwithstanding this death-bed confession, most people doubted the truth of the relation, from his general character, and other circumstances.

" articles, which they may find belonging to those people.—The
" natives will be made severe examples of whenever any man is
" wounded by them : but this will be done in a manner which
" may satisfy them, that it is a punishment inflicted on them for
" their own bad conduct, and of which they cannot be made sen-
" sible, if they are not treated with kindness, while they continue
" peaceable and quiet.

" A party, consisting of two captains, two subalterns, and forty
" privates, with a proper number of non-commissioned officers,
" from the garrison, with three days provisions, &c. are to be
" ready to march to-morrow morning at day-light, in order to
" bring in six of those natives who reside near the head of Botany
" Bay ; or, if that should be found impracticable, to put that
" number to death."

Just previous to this order being issued, the author of this publication received a direction to attend the governor at head quarters
immediately. I went, and his excellency informed me, that he had
pitched upon me to execute the foregoing command. He added,
that the two subalterns who were to be drawn from the marine
corps, should be chosen by myself : that the serjeant, and the
two convicts who were with M'Entire, should attend as guides :
that we were to proceed to the peninsula at the head of Botany
Bay ; and thence, or from any part of the north arm of the bay,
we were, if practicable, to bring away two natives as prisoners :
and to put to death ten : that we were to destroy all weapons of
war, but nothing else : that no hut was to be burned : that all
women and children were to remain uninjured, not being comprehended within the scope of the order : that our operations were
to be directed, either by surprize, or open force : that after we had
made any prisoners, all communication, even with those natives
with whom we were in habits of intercourse, was to be avoided,

and none of them suffered to approach us.—That we were to cut off, and bring in the heads of the slain, for which purpose, hatchets and bags would be furnished.—And finally, that no signal of amity or invitation should be used, in order to allure them to us; or if made on their part, to be answered by us: for that such conduct would be not only present treachery, but give them reason to distrust every future mark of peace and friendship on our part.

December, 1790. His excellency was now pleased to enter into the reasons which had induced him to adopt measures of such severity. He said that since our arrival in the country, no less than seventeen of our people had either been killed or wounded by the natives:—that he looked upon the tribe known by the name of Bid-ee-gàl, living on the beforementioned peninsula, and chiefly on the north arm of Botany Bay, to be the principal aggressors:—that against this tribe he was determined to strike a decisive blow, in order, at once to convince them of our superiority, and to infuse an universal terror, which might operate to prevent farther mischief.—That his observations on the natives had led him to conclude, that although they did not fear death individually, yet that the relative weight and importance of the different tribes appeared to be the highest object of their estimation, as each tribe deemed its strength and security to consist wholly in its powers, aggregately considered.—That his motive for having so long delayed to use violent measures, had arisen from believing, that in every former instance of hostility, they had acted either from having received injury, or from misapprehension. " To the latter of these " causes," added he, " I attribute my own wound; but in this bu- " siness of M'Entire, I am fully persuaded that they were unpro- " voked, and the barbarity of their conduct admits of no extenua- " tion: for I have separately examined the serjeant, of whose ve-

" racity I have the highest opinion, and the two convicts; and
" their story is short, simple, and alike. I have in vain tried to
" stimulate Baneelon, Colbee, and the other natives who live
" among us, to bring in the aggressor: yesterday, indeed, they
" promised me to do it, and actually went away, as if bent on such
" a design; but Baneelon, instead of directing his steps to Botany
" Bay, crossed the harbour in his canoe, in order to draw the fore-
" teeth of some of the young men; and Colbee, in the room of
" fulfilling his engagement, is loitering about the look-out house.
" Nay, so far from wishing even to describe faithfully the person of
" the man who has thrown the spear, they pretended that he has
" a distorted foot, which is a palpable falsehood. So that we have
" our efforts only to depend upon; and I am resolved to execute
" the prisoners who may be brought in, in the most public and ex-
" emplary manner, in the presence of as many of their countrymen
" as can be collected, after having explained the cause of such a
" punishment; and my fixed determination to repeat it, whenever
" any future breach of good conduct on their side, shall render it
" necessary."

Here the governor stopped, and addressing himself to me, said,
if I could propose any alteration of the orders under which I was
to act, he would patiently listen to me: encouraged by this condescension, I begged leave to offer for consideration, whether, instead of destroying ten persons, the capture of six would not better answer all the purposes for which the expedition was to be undertaken; as out of this number, a part might be set aside for retaliation; and the rest, at a proper time, liberated, after having
seen the fate of their comrades, and being made sensible of the
cause of their own detention.

December, 1790. This scheme, his excellency was pleased instantly to adopt, adding, " if six cannot be taken, let this number

" be shot. Should you, however, find it practicable to take so
" many, I will hang two, and send the rest to Norfolk Island for
" a certain period, which will cause their countrymen to believe,
" that we have dispatched them secretly." The order was accordingly altered to its present form; and I took my leave to prepare,
after being again cautioned not to deceive, by holding signals of
amity.

At four o'clock on the morning of the 14th we marched: the
detachment consisted, besides myself, of captain Hill of the New
South Wales corps, lieutenants Poulden and Dawes, of the marines, Mr. Worgan and Mr. Lowes, surgeons, three serjeants,
three corporals, and forty private soldiers, provided with three
days provisions, ropes to bind our prisoners with, and hatchets and
bags, to cut off and contain the heads of the slain. By nine o'clock
this terrific procession reached the peninsula, at the head of Botany Bay; but after having walked in various directions until four
o'clock in the afternoon, without seeing a native, we halted for the
night.

At daylight on the following morning our search recommenced.
We marched in an easterly direction, intending to fall in with the
south-west arm of the bay, about three miles above its mouth,
which we determined to scour, and thence passing along the head
of the peninsula, to proceed to the north arm, and complete our
search. However, by a mistake of our guides, at half past seven
o'clock, instead of finding ourselves on the south-west arm, we
came suddenly upon the sea shore, at the head of the peninsula,
about midway between the two arms. Here we saw five Indians
on the beach, whom we attempted to surround; but they penetrated our design, and before we could get near enough to effect
our purpose, ran off. We pursued; but a contest between heavy-
armed Europeans, fettered by ligatures, and naked unencumbered

Indians, was too unequal to last long. They darted into the wood and disappeared.

December, 1790. The alarm being given, we were sensible that no hope of success remained, but by a rapid movement to a little village (if five huts deserve the name,) which we knew stood on the nearest point of the north arm, where possibly some one unapprized of our approach, might yet be found. Thither we hastened ; but before we could reach it three canoes, filled with Indians, were seen paddling over in the utmost hurry and trepredation, to the opposite shore, where universal alarm prevailed. All we could now do was to search the huts for weapons of war : but we found nothing except fish gigs, which we left untouched.

On our return to our baggage (which we had left behind under a small guard near the place where the pursuit had begun) we observed a native fishing in shallow water not higher than his waist, at the distance of 300 yards from the land. In such a situation it would not have been easily practicable either to shoot, or seize him. I therefore determined to pass without noticing him, as he seemed either from consciousness of his own security, or from some other cause, quite unintimidated at our appearance. At length he called to several of us by name, and in spite of our formidable array, drew nearer with unbounded confidence. Surprized at his behaviour I ordered a halt, that he might overtake us, fully resolved, whoever he might be, that he should be suffered to come to us and leave us uninjured. Presently we found it to be our friend Colbee ; and he joined us at once with his wonted familiarity and unconcern. We asked him where Pimelwi was, and found that he perfectly comprehended the nature of our errand, for he described him to have fled to the southward ; and to be at such a distance, as, had we known the account to be true, would have prevented our going in search of him, without a fresh supply of provisions.

When we arrived at our baggage, Colbee sat down, eat, drank, and slept with us, from ten o'clock until past noon. We asked him several questions about Sydney, which he had left on the preceding day ;* and told us he had been present at an operation performed at the hospital, where Mr. White had cut off a woman's leg. The agony and cries of the poor sufferer he depicted in a most lively manner.

At one o'clock we renewed our march, and at three halted near a fresh water swamp, where we resolved to remain until morning: that is, after a day of severe fatigue, to pass a night of restless inquietude, when weariness is denied repose by swarms of musquitoes and sand-flies, which in the summer months bite and sting the traveller, without measure or intermission.

Next morning we bent our steps homeward ; and, after wading breast-high through two arms of the sea, as broad as the Thames at Westminster, were glad to find ourselves at Sydney, between one and two o'clock in the afternoon.

The few remarks which I was able to make on the country through which we had passed, were such as will not tempt adventurers to visit it on the score of pleasure or advantage. The soil of every part of the peninsula, which we had traversed, is shallow and

---

* He had it seems visited the governor about noon, after having gained information from Nanbaree of our march, and for what purpose it was undertaken. This he did not scruple to tell to the governor ; proclaiming at the same time, a resolution of going to Botany Bay, which his excellency endeavoured to dissuade him from by every argument he could devise : a blanket, a hatchet, a jacket, or aught else he would ask for, was offered to him in vain, if he would not go. At last it was determined to try to *eat him down,* by setting before him his favourite food, of which it was hoped he would feed so voraciously, as to render him incapable of executing his intention. A large dish of fish was accordingly set before him. But after devouring a light horseman, and at least five pounds of beef and bread, even until the sight of food became disgusting to him, he set out on his journey with such lightness and gaiety, as plainly shewed him to be a stranger to the horrors of indigestion.

sandy, and its productions meagre and wretched. When forced to quit the sand, we were condemned to drag through morasses, or to clamber over rocks, unrefreshed by streams, and unmarked by diversity. Of the soil I brought away several specimens.

Our first expedition having so totally failed, the governor resolved to try the fate of a second ; and the ' painful pre-eminence' again devolved on me.

December, 1790. The orders under which I was commanded to act differing in no respect from the last, I resolved to try once more to surprise the village beforementioned. And in order to deceive the natives, and prevent them from again frustrating our design by promulging it, we feigned that our preparations were directed against Broken Bay ; and that the man who had wounded the governor was the object of punishment. It was now also determined, being full moon, that our operations should be carried on in the night, both for the sake of secrecy, and for avoiding the extreme heat of the day.

A little before sun-set on the evening of the 22d, we marched. Lieutenant Abbot, and ensign Prentice, of the New South Wales corps, were the two officers under my command, and with three serjeants, three corporals, and thirty privates, completed the detachment.

We proceeded directly to the fords of the north arm of Botany Bay, which we had crossed in our last expedition, on the banks of which we were compelled to wait until a quarter past two in the morning, for the ebb of the tide. As these passing-places consist only of narrow slips of ground, on each side of which are dangerous holes ; and as fording rivers in the night is at all times an unpleasant task, I determined before we entered the water, to disburthen the men as much as possible ; that in case of stepping wrong every one might be as ready, as circumstances would admit, to recover himself. The firelock and cartouche-box were all that we carried, the latter tied fast on the top of the head, to prevent it from being wetted. The knapsacks, &c. I left in charge of a serjeant and six men, who from their low stature and other causes, were most likely to impede our march, the success of which I knew hinged on our ability, by a rapid movement, to surprize the village before day-break.

The two rivers were crossed without any material accident: and in pursuit of my resolution, I ordered the guides to conduct us by the nearest route, without heeding difficulty, or impediment of road. Having continued to push along the river-bank very briskly for three quarters of an hour, we were suddenly stopped by a creek, about sixty yards wide, which extended to our right, and appeared dry from the tide being out: I asked if it could be passed, or whether it would be better to wheel round the head of it. Our guides answered that it was bad to cross, but might be got over, which would save us more than a quarter of a mile. Knowing the value of time, I directly bade them to push through, and every one began to follow as well as he could. They who were foremost had not, however, got above half over when the difficulty of progress was sensibly experienced. We were immersed, nearly to the waist in mud, so thick and tenacious, that it was not without the most vigorous exertion of every muscle of the body, that the legs could be disengaged. When we had reached the middle, our distress became not only more pressing, but serious, and each succeeding step, buried us deeper. At length a serjeant of grenadiers stuck fast, and declared himself incapable of moving either forward or backward; and just after, ensign Prentice, and I, felt ourselves in a similar predicament, close together. 'I find it impossible to move; I am sinking;' resounded on every side. What to do I knew not: every moment brought increase of perplexity, and augmented danger, as those who could not proceed kept gradually subsiding. From our misfortunes, however, those in the rear profited. Warned by what they saw and heard, they inclined to the right towards the head of the creek, and thereby contrived to pass over.

December, 1790. Our distress would have terminated fatally, had not a soldier cried out to those on shore to cut boughs of trees,* and throw them to us: a lucky thought, which certainly saved many of us from perishing miserably ; and even with this assistance, had we been burdened by our knapsacks, we could not have emerged ; for it employed us near half an hour to disentangle some of our number. The serjeant of grenadiers in particular, was sunk to his breast-bone, and so firmly fixed in, that the efforts of many men were required to extricate him, which was effected in the moment after I had ordered one of the ropes, destined to bind the captive Indians, to be fastened under his arms.

Having congratulated each other on our escape from this ‘ Serbonian Bog,’ and wiped our arms (half of which were rendered unserviceable by the mud) we once more pushed forward to our object, within a few hundred yards of which, we found ourselves about half an hour before sunrise. Here I formed the detachment into three divisions, and having enjoined the most perfect silence, in order, if possible, to deceive Indian vigilance, each division was directed to take a different route, so as to meet at the village at the same moment.

We rushed rapidly on, and nothing could succeed more exactly than the arrival of the several detachments. To our astonishment, however, we found not a single native at the huts ; nor was a canoe to be seen on any part of the bay. I was at first inclined

---

* I had often read of this contrivance to facilitate the passage of a morass. But I confess, that in my confusion I had entirely forgotten it, and probably should have continued to do so until too late to be of use.

to attribute this to our arriving half an hour too late, from the numberless impediments we had encountered. But on closer exa-mination, there appeared room to believe, that many days had elapsed since an Indian had been on the spot, as no mark of fresh fires, or fish-bones, was to be found.

Disappointed and fatigued, we would willingly have profited by the advantage of being near water, and have halted to refresh. But on consultation, it was found, that unless we reached in an hour the rivers we had so lately passed, it would be impossible, on account of the tide, to cross to our baggage, in which case we should be without food until evening. We therefore pushed back, and by dint of alternately running and walking, arrived at the fords time enough to pass with ease and safety. So excessive, however, had been our efforts, and so laborious our progress, that several of the soldiers, in the course of the last two miles, gave up, and confessed themselves unable to proceed farther. All that I could do for these poor fellows, was to order their comrades to carry their mus-kets, and to leave with them a small party of those men who were least exhausted, to assist them, and hurry them on. In three quarters of an hour after we had crossed the water, they arrived at it, just time enough to effect a passage.

The necessity of repose, joined to the succeeding heat of the day, induced us to prolong our halt until four o'clock in the afternoon, when we recommenced our operations on the opposite side of the north arm to that we had acted upon in the morning. Our march ended at sun-set, without our seeing a single native. We had passed through the country, which the discoverers of Botany Bay extol as ' *some of the finest meadows in the world.*'* These meadows,

* The words which are quoted may be found in Mr. Cook's first voyage, and form part of his description of Botany Bay. It has often fallen to my lot to traverse these fabled plains ; and many a bitter execration have I heard poured on those travellers, who could so faithlessly relate what they saw.

instead of grass, are covered with high coarse rushes, growing in a rotten spungy bog, into which we were plunged knee-deep at every step.

Our final effort was made at half past one o'clock next morning ; and after four hours toil, ended as those preceding it had done, in disappointment and vexation. At nine o'clock we returned to Sydney, to report our fruitless peregrination.

December, 1790. But if we could not retaliate on the murderer of M'Entire, we found no difficulty in punishing offences committed within our own observation. Two natives, about this time, were detected in robbing a potatoe garden ; when seen, they ran away, and a serjeant and a party of soldiers were dispatched in pursuit of them. Unluckily it was dark when they overtook them, with some women at a fire ; and the ardour of the soldiers transported them so far, that, instead of capturing the offenders, they fired in among them. The women were taken, but the two men escaped.

On the following day, blood was traced from the fire-place to the sea-side, where it seemed probable, that those who had lost it, had embarked. The natives were observed to become immediately shy ; but an exact knowledge of the mischief which had been committed, was not gained until the end of two days, when they said, that a man of the name of Ban g-ai (who was known to be one of the pilferers) was wounded and dead. Imeerawanyee, however, whispered, that though he was wounded, he was not dead. A hope now existed, that his life might be saved ; and Mr. White, taking Imeerawanyee, Narbaree, and a woman with him, set out for the spot where he was reported to be. But on their reaching it, they were told by some people who were there, that the man was dead, and that the corpse was deposited in a bay about a mile off. Thither they accordingly repaired, and found it as described, covered, except one leg, which seemed to be designedly left bare, with green boughs, and a fire burning near it. Those who had performed the funeral obsequies, seemed to have been particularly solicitous for the protection of the face, which was covered with a thick branch, interwoven with grass and fern, so as to form a complete screen. Around the neck was a strip of the bark, of which they make fishing lines, and a young strait stick growing near, was stripped of its bark, and bent down so as to form an arch over the body, in which position it was confined by a forked branch stuck into the earth.

December, 1790. On examining the corpse, it was found to be warm. Through the shoulder had passed a musquet ball, which had divided the subclavian artery, and caused death, by loss of blood ; no mark of any remedy having been applied could be discovered. Possibly the nature of the wound, which even among us, would baffle cure without amputation of the arm at the shoulder, was deemed so fatal, that they despaired of success, and therefore left it to itself. Had Mr. White found the man alive, there is little room to think that he could have been of any use to him ; for that an Indian would submit to so formidable and alarming an operation seems hardly probable.

None of the natives who had come in the boat would touch the body, or even go near it, saying, the *Mawn* would come ; that is literally, *the spirit of the deceased would seize them.* Of the people who died among us, they had expressed no such apprehension. But how far the difference of a natural death, and one effected by violence, may operate on their fears to induce superstition ; and why those who had performed the rites of sepulture, should not experience similar fears and reluctance, I leave to be determined. Certain it is (as I shall insist upon more hereafter), that they believe the spirit of the dead not to be extinct with the body.

Baneelon took an odd method of revenging the death of his countryman: at the head of several of his tribe, he robbed one of the private boats of fish, threatening the people, who were unarmed, that in case they resisted, he would spear them. On being taxed by the governor with this outrage, he at first stoutly denied it: but on being confronted with the people who were in the boat, he changed his language, and, without deigning even to palliate his offence, burst into fury, and demanded who had killed *Bangäi*.

CHAPTER XIII.

The Transactions of the Colony continued to the End of May, 1791.

December, 1790. THE Dutch snow from Batavia arrived on the 17th of the month, after a passage of twelve weeks, in which she had lost sixteen of her people. But death, to a man who has resided at Batavia, is too familiar an object to excite either terror or regret. All the people of the Supply, who were left there sick, except one midshipman, had also perished in that fatal climate.

The cargo of the snow consisted chiefly of rice, with a small quantity of beef, pork, and flour.

A letter was received by this vessel, written by the *Shebander,* at Batavia, to governor Phillip, acquainting him, that war had commenced between England and Spain. As this letter was written in the Dutch language, we did not find it easy of translation. It filled us, however, with anxious perturbation, and with wishes as impotent, as they were eager, in the cause of our country. Though far beyond the din of arms, we longed to contribute to her glory, and to share in her triumphs.

Placed out of the reach of attack, both by remoteness and insignificancy, our only dread lay lest those supplies intended for our consumption, should be captured. Not, however, to be found totally unprovided, in case an enemy should appear, a battery was planned near the entrance of Sydney Cove, and other formidable preparations set on foot.

The commencement of the year 1791, though marked by no cir-

P

cumstances particularly favourable, beamed far less inauspicious than that of 1790 had done.

January, 1791. No circumstance, however apparently trivial, which can tend to throw light on a new country, either in respect of its present situation, or its future promise, should pass unregarded.—On the 24th of January, two bunches of grapes were cut in the governor's garden, from cuttings of vines, brought three years before from the Cape of Good Hope. The bunches were handsome; the fruit of a moderate size, but well filled out; and the flavour high and delicious

The first step after unloading the Dutch snow, was to dispatch the Supply to Norfolk Island, for captain Hunter, and the crew of the Sirius, who had remained there ever since the loss of that ship. It had always been the governor's wish to hire the Dutchman, 'for the purpose of transporting them to England. But the frantic extravagant behaviour of the master of her, for a long time frustrated the conclusion of a contract. He was so totally lost to a sense of reason and propriety, as to ask *eleven pounds* per ton, monthly, for her use, until she should arrive *from England, at Batavia*. This was treated with proper contempt; and he was at last induced to accept *twenty shillings* a ton, per month, (rating her at three hundred tons) until she should arrive *in England :*— being about the twenty-fifth part of his original demand. And even at this price, she was, perhaps, the dearest vessel ever hired on a similar service, being totally destitute of every accommodation, and every good quality, which could promise to render so long a voyage, either comfortable or expeditious.

February, 1791. On the 26th, captain Hunter, his officers, and ship's company, joined us; and on the 28th of March, the snow sailed with them for England; intending to make a northern passage by Timor and Batavia; the season being too far advanced to render the southern route by Cape Horn practicable.*

Six days previous to the departure of captain Hunter, the indefatigable Supply again sailed for Norfolk Island, carrying thither captain Hill, and a detachment of the New South Wales corps. A little native boy, named *Bòn-del,* who had long particularly attached himself to captain Hill, accompanied him, at his own earnest request. His father had been killed in battle, and his mother bitten in two by a shark: so that he was an orphan, dependant on the humanity of his tribe for protection.† His disappearance seemed to make no impression on the rest of his countrymen, who were apprized of his resolution to go. On the return of the Supply, they inquired eagerly for him; and on being told that the place he was gone to afforded plenty of birds and other good fare, innumerable volunteers presented themselves to follow him;—so great was their confidence in us, and so little hold of them had the *amor patriæ.*

March, 1791. The snow had but just sailed, when a very daring manœuvre was carried into execution, with complete success, by a set of convicts, eleven in number, including a woman, wife of one of the party, and two little children. They seized the governor's cutter; and putting into her a seine, fishing-lines, and hooks, fire-arms, a quadrant, compass, and some provisions, boldly pushed out to sea, determined to brave every danger, and combat every hardship, rather than remain longer in a captive state. Most of these people had been brought out in the first fleet; and the terms of transportation of some of them were expired. Among them were a fisherman, a carpenter, and some competent naviga-

---

* They did not arrive in England until April, 1792.

† I am of opinion that such protection is always extended to children who may be left destitute.

tors ; so that little doubt was entertained, that a scheme so admirably planned, would be adequately executed. * When their elopement was discovered, a pursuit was ordered by the governor. But
the fugitives had made too good an use of the intermediate time,
to be even seen by their pursuers. After the escape of captain
Bligh, which was well known to us, no length of passage, or hazard of navigation, seemed above human accomplishment. However to prevent future attempts of a like nature, the governor directed, that boats only of stated dimensions, should be built. Indeed an order of this sort had been issued on the escape of the first
party ; and it was now repeated with additional restrictions.

April, 1791. Notwithstanding the supplies which had recently
arrived from Batavia, short allowance was again proclaimed on
the 2d of April, on which day we were reduced to the following
ration:

Three pounds of rice, three pounds of flour, and three pounds of
pork, per week.

* It was my fate to fall in again with part of this little band of adventurers. In March
1792, when I arrived in the Gorgon, at the Cape of Good Hope, six of these people, including the woman and one child, were put on board of us, to be carried to England : four had
died, and one had jumped overboard at Batavia. The particulars of their voyage were
briefly as follows. They coasted the shore of New Holland, putting occasionally into different
harbours which they found in going along. One of these harbours, in the latitude of 30°
south, they described to be of superior excellence and capacity. Here they hauled their bark
ashore, paid her seams with tallow, and repaired her. But it was with difficulty they could
keep off the attacks of the Indians. These people continued to harras them so much, that
they quitted the main land and retreated to a small island in the harbour, where they completed their design. Between the latitude of 26° and 27°, they were driven by a current 30
leagues from the shore, among some islands, where they found plenty of large turtles. Soon
after they closed again with the continent, when the boat got entangled in the surf, and was
driven on shore, and they had all well nigh perished. They passed through the straits of Endeavour, and beyond the gulf of Carpentaria found a large fresh water river, which they entered and filled from it their empty casks.

Until they reached the gulf of Carpentaria, they saw no natives, or canoes, differing from
those about Port Jackson. But now they were chased by large canoes, fitted with sails

It was singularly unfortunate that these retrenchments should always happen when the gardens were most destitute of vegetables. A long drought had nearly exhausted them. The hardships which we in consequence suffered, were great; but not comparable to what had been formerly experienced. Besides, now we made sure of ships arriving soon to dispel our distress: whereas, heretofore, from having never heard from England, the hearts of men sunk; and many had begun to doubt, whether it had not been resolved to try how long misery might be endured with resignation.

Notwithstanding the incompetency of so diminished a pittance, the daily task of the soldier and convict continued unaltered. I never contemplated the labours of these men, without finding abundant cause of reflection on the miseries which our nature can overcome.—Let me for a moment quit the cold track of narrative: —let me not fritter away by servile adaptation, those reflections, and

and fighting stages, and capable of holding thirty men each. They escaped by dint of rowing to windward. On the 5th of June 1791, they reached Timor, and pretended that they had belonged to a ship, which, on her passage from Port Jackson to India, had foundered ; and that they only had escaped. The Dutch received them with kindness, and treated them with hospitality ? but their behaviour giving rise to suspicion, they were watched ; and one of them at last, in a moment of intoxication, betrayed the secret. They were immediately secured, and committed to prison. Soon after captain Edwards of the Pandora, who had been wrecked near Endeavour straits, arrived at Timor, and they were delivered up to him, by which means they became passengers in the Gorgon.

I confess that I never looked at these people, without pity and astonishment. They had miscarried in a heroic struggle for liberty ; after having combated every hardship, and conquered every difficulty.

The woman, and one of the men, had gone out to Port Jackson in the ship which had transported me thither. They had both of them been always distinguished for good behaviour. And I could not but reflect with admiration, at the strange combination of circumstances which had again brought us together, to baffle human foresight, and confound human speculation.

the feelings they gave birth to:—let me transcribe them fresh as they arose, ardent and generous, though hopeless and romantic.— I every day see wretches pale with disease and wasted with famine, struggle against the horrors of their situation. How striking is the effect of subordination; how dreadful is the fear of punishment!—The allotted task is still performed, even on the present reduced subsistence:—the blacksmith sweats at the sultry forge; the sawyer labours pent-up in his pit; and the husbandman turns up the sterile glebe.—Shall I again hear arguments multiplied to violate truth, and insult humanity!—Shall I again be told that the sufferings of the wretched Africans are indispensable for the culture of our sugar colonies: that white men are incapable of sustaining the heat of the climate!—I have been in the West Indies:— I have lived there.—I know that it is a rare instance for the mercury in the thermometer to mount there above 90°; and here I scarcely pass a week in summer without seeing it rise to 100°; sometimes to 105; nay, beyond even that burning altitude.

But toil cannot be long supported without adequate refreshment. The first step in every community, which wishes to preserve honesty, should be to set the people above want. The *throes* of hunger will ever prove too powerful for integrity to withstand. —Hence arose a repetition of petty delinquencies, which no vigilance could detect, and no justice reach. Gardens were plundered; provisions pilfered; and the Indian corn stolen from the fields, where it grew for public use. Various were the measures adopted to check this depredatory spirit. Criminal courts, either from the tediousness of their process, or from the frequent escape of culprits from their decision, were seldomer convened than formerly. The governor ordered convict-offenders either to be chained together; or to wear singly a large iron collar, with two spikes projecting from it, which effectually hindered the party from concealing it under his shirt: and thus shackled, they were compelled to perform their quota of work.

May, 1791. Had their marauding career terminated here, humanity would have been anxious to plead in their defence: but the natives continued to complain of being robbed of spears, and fishing tackle. A convict was at length taken in the fact of stealing fishing-tackle from Dar-in-ga, the wife of Colbee. The governor ordered that he should be severely flogged, in the presence of as many natives as could be assembled, to whom the cause of punishment should be explained. Many of them, of both sexes, accordingly attended. Arabanoo's aversion to a similar sight has been noticed: and if the behaviour of those now collected be found to correspond with it; it is, I think, fair to conclude, that these people are not of a sanguinary and implacable temper. Quick indeed of resentment, but not unforgiving of injury. There was not one of them that did not testify strong abhorrence of the punishment, and equal sympathy with the sufferer. The women were particularly affected; Daringa shed tears; and Barangaroo, kindling into anger, snatched a stick, and menaced the executioner. The conduct of these women, on this occasion, was exactly descriptive of their characters. The former was ever meek and feminine; the latter, fierce and unsubmissive.

1791. On the first of May, many allotments of ground were parcelled out by the governor to convicts, whose periods of transportation were expired, and who voluntarily offered to become settlers in the country. The terms on which they settled, and their progress in agriculture, will be hereafter set forth.

CHAPTER. XIV.

Travelling Diaries in New South Wales.

FROM among my numerous travelling journals into the interior parts of the country, I select the following, to present to the reader, as equally important in their object, and more amusing in their detail, than any other.

In April, 1791, an expedition was undertaken, in order to ascertain whether or not the Hawkesbury and the Nepean, were the same river. With this view, we proposed to fall in a little above Richmond Hill,* and trace down to it ; and if the weather should prove fine, to cross at the ford, and go a short distance westward, then to repass the river, and trace it upward, until we should either arrive at some spot which we knew to be the Nepean, or should determine by its course, that the Hawkesbury was a different stream.

1791.   Our party was strong and numerous : it consisted of twenty-one persons, viz. The governor, Mr. Collins and his servant, Mr. White, Mr. Dawes, the author, three gamekeepers, two serjeants, eight privates, and our friends Colbee and Boladeree.   These two last were volunteers on the occasion, on being assured that we should not stay out many days, and that we should carry plenty of provisions.   Baneelon wished to go, but his wife would not permit it.   Colbee, on the other hand, would listen to

---

* Look at the map for the situation of this place.

no objections. He only stipulated (with great care and consideration) that during his absence, his wife and child should remain at
Sydney under our protection, and be supplied with provisions.

But before we set out, let me describe our equipment, and try to
convey to those who have rolled along on turnpike roads only, an
account of those preparations which are required in traversing the
wilderness.—Every man (the governor excepted) carried his own
knapsack, which contained provisions for ten days; if to this be
added, a gun, a blanket, and a canteen, the weight will fall nothing short of forty pounds. Slung to the knapsack, are the
cooking kettle, and the hatchet, with which the wood to kindle
the nightly fire, and build the nightly hut, is to be cut down.
Garbed to drag through morasses, tear through thickets, ford
rivers, and scale rocks; our autumnal heroes, who annually
seek the hills in pursuit of grouse and black game, afford but an
imperfect representation of the picture.

Thus encumbered, the march begins at sunrise, and with occa-
sional halts,continues until about an hour and a half before sunset.
It is necessary to stop thus early to prepare for passing the night,
for toil here ends not with the march. Instead of the cheering blaze,
the welcoming landlord, and the long bill of fare, the traveller
has now to collect his fuel, to erect his wigwam, to fetch water,
and to broil his morsel of salt pork. Let him then lie down, and
if it be summer, try whether the effect of fatigue is sufficiently
powerful to overcome the bites and stings of the myriads of sand
flies and musquitoes, which buz around him.

Monday, April 11, 1791. At twenty minutes before seven o'clock,
we started from the governor's house at Rose Hill, and steered *

* Our method, on these expeditions, was to steer by compass, noting the different
courses as we proceeded; and counting the number of paces, of which two thousand two

for a short time nearly in a north-east direction; after which we turned to north 34° west, and steadily pursued that course until a quarter before four o'clock, when we halted for the night. The country for the first two miles, while we walked to the north-east, was good, full of grass, and without rock or underwood; afterwards it grew very bad, being full of steep barren rocks, over which we were compelled to clamber for seven miles, when it changed to a plain country, apparently very sterile, and with very little grass in it, which rendered walking easy. Our fatigue in the morning had, however, been so oppressive, that one of the party *knocked up*. And had not a soldier, as strong as a pack-horse, undertaken to carry his knapsack, in addition to his own, we must either have sent him back, or have stopped at a place for the night which did not afford water. Our two natives carried each his pack, but its weight was inconsiderable, most of their provisions being in the knapsacks of the soldiers and gamekeepers. We expected to have derived from them much information relating to the country; as no one doubted that they were acquainted with every part of it between the sea-coast and the river Hawkesbury. We hoped also to have witnessed their manner of living in the woods, and the resources they rely upon in their journies. Nothing, however, of this sort had yet occurred, except their examining some trees, to see if they

hundred, on good ground, were allowed to be a mile. At night when we halted, all these courses were separately cast up, and worked by a traverse table, in the manner a ship's reckoning is kept; so that by observing this precaution, we always knew exactly where we were, and how far from home: an unspeakable advantage in a new country, where one hill, and one tree, is so like another, that fatal wanderings would ensue without it. This arduous task was always allotted to Mr. Dawes, who, from habit and superior skill, performed it almost without a stop, or an interruption of conversation: to any other man, on such terms, it would have been impracticable.

could discover on the bark any marks of the claws of squirrels and oppossums, which they said would shew whether any of those animals were hidden among the leaves and branches. They walked stoutly, appeared but little fatigued, and maintained their spirits admirably, laughing to excess when any of us either tripped or stumbled; misfortunes which much seldomer fell to their lot than to ours. At a very short distance from Rose Hill, we found that they were in a country unknown to them ; so that the farther they went, the more dependant on us they became, being absolute strangers inland. To convey to their understandings the intention of our journey, was impossible. For, perhaps, no words could unfold to an Indian, the motives of curiosity, which induce men to encounter labour, fatigue, and pain, when they might remain in repose at home, with a sufficiency of food.—We asked Colbee the name of the people who live inland, and he called them Boò-roo-ber-on-gal ; and said, they were bad ; whence we conjectured, that they sometimes war with those on the sea coast, by whom they were undoubtedly driven up the country from the fishing ground, that it might not be overstocked : the weaker here, as in every other country, giving way to the stronger. We asked how they lived. He said, on birds and animals, having no fish. Their laziness appeared strongly when we halted ; for they refused to draw water, or to cleave wood to make a fire ; but as soon as it was kindled (having first well stuffed themselves), they lay down before it and fell asleep. About an hour after sunset, as we were chatting by the fire side, and preparing to go to rest, we heard voices at a little distance in the wood. Our natives catched the sound instantaneously, and bidding us be silent, listened attentively to the quarter whence it had proceeded. In a few minutes we heard the voices plainly ; and wishing exceedingly to open a communication with this tribe, we begged our natives to call to them, and bid them to

Q 2

come to us, to assure them of good treatment, and that they should have something given them to eat. Colbee no longer hesitated, but gave them the signal of invitation, in a loud hollow cry After some whooping, and shouting, on both sides, a man, with a lighted stick in his hand, advanced near enough to converse with us. The first words, which we could distinctly understand were, ' I am Colbee, of the tribe of Càd-i-gal.' The stranger replied, ' I am Bèr-ee-wan, ' of the tribe of Boorooberongal.' Boladeree informed him also of his name, and that we were white men and friends, who would give him something to eat. Still he seemed irresolute. Colbee therefore advanced to him, took him by the hand, and led him to us. By the light of the moon, we were introduced to this gentleman, all our names being repeated in form by our two masters of the ceremonies, who said that we were Englishmen, and *Bùd-ye-ree* (good), that we came from the sea coast, and that we were travelling inland. Bereewan seemed to be a man about thirty years old, differing in no respect from his countrymen with whom we were acquainted. He came to us unarmed, having left his spears at a little distance. After a long conversation with his countrymen, and having received some provisions, he departed highly satisfied.

Tuesday, April 12*th*, 1791. Started this morning at half past six o'clock, and in two hours reached the river. The whole of the country we passed was poor, and the soil within a mile of the river changed to a coarse deep sand, which I have invariably found to compose its banks, in every part, without exception, that I ever saw. The stream at this place is about three hundred and fifty feet wide; the water pure and excellent to the taste; the banks are about twenty feet high, and covered with trees, many of which had been evidently bent by the force of the current, in the direction which it runs, and some of them contained rubbish and drift wood in their branches, at least forty-five feet above the level of the stream. We saw many ducks, and killed one, which Colbee swam for. No new production among the shrubs growing here was found: we were acquainted with them all. Our natives had evidently never seen this river before: they stared at it with surprise, and talked to each other. Their total ignorance of the country, and of the direction in which they had walked, appeared, when they were asked which way Rose Hill lay; for they pointed almost oppositely to it. Of our compass they had taken early notice, and had talked much to each other about it: they comprehended its use; and called it " *Naa-Moro,*" literally, " *To see the way*;—a more significant or expressive term cannot be found.

April, 1791. Supposing ourselves to be higher on the stream than Richmond Hill, we agreed to trace downward, or to the right hand.—In tracing, we kept as close to the bank of the river, as the innumerable impediments to walking which grow upon it, would allow. We found the country low and swampy: came to a native fire-place, at which were some small fish-bones: soon after we saw a native, but he ran away immediately. Having walked nearly three miles we were stopped by a creek which we could neither ford, or fall a tree across: we were therefore obliged to coast it, in hope to find a passing place, or to reach its head At four o'clock we halted for the night, on the bank of the creek. —Our natives continued to hold out stoutly. The hindrances to walking by the river side, which plagued and entangled us so much, seemed not to be heeded by them, and they wound through them with ease; but to us they were intolerably tiresome. Our perplexities afforded them an inexhaustible fund of merriment and derision:—did the sufferer, stung at once with nettles and ridicule, and shaken nigh to death by his fall, use any angry expression to them, they retorted in a moment, by calling him by every opprobrious name* which their language affords.—Boladerree destroyed

* Their general favourite term of reproach is *Go-nin-Pat-ta,* which signifies, *an eater of*

a native hut to-day very wantonly, before we could prevent him. On being asked why he did so, he answered, that the inhabitants inland were bad; though no longer since than last night, when Bereewan had departed, they were loud in their praise. But now they had reverted to their first opinion:—so fickle and transient are their motives of love and hatred.

Wednesday, April 13th, 1791. We did not set out this morning until past seven o'clock, when we continued to trace the creek. The country which we passed through yesterday was good and desirable to what was now presented to us: it was in general high, and universally rocky. " Toiling our uncouth way," we mounted a hill, and surveyed the contiguous country. To the northward and eastward, the ground was still higher than that we were upon; but in a south-west direction we saw about four miles: the view consisted of nothing but trees growing on precipices; not an acre of it could be cultivated.—Saw a tree on fire here, and several other vestiges of the natives. To comprehend the reasons which induce an Indian to perform many of the offices of life is difficult: to pronounce that which could lead him to wander amidst these dreary wilds, baffles penetration. About two o'clock we reached the head of the creek; passed it, and scrambled with infinite toil and difficulty to the top of a neighbouring mountain, whence we saw the adjacent country, in almost every direction, for many miles. I record with regret that this extended view presented not a single gleam of change, which could encourage hope, or stimulate industry, to attempt its culture. We had, however, the satisfaction to discover plainly the object of our pursuit, Richmond Hill, distant about eight miles, in a *contrary* direction from what we had been proceeding upon. It was readily known to those who had been

human excrement.—Our language would admit a very concise and familiar translation. They have, besides this, innumerable others, which they often salute their enemies with.

up the Hawkesbury in the boats, by a remarkable cleft or notch which distinguishes it. It was now determined that we should go back to the head of the creek, and pass the night there; and in the morning cut across the country to that part of the river which we had first hit upon yesterday, and thence to trace upward, or to the left.—But, before I descend, I must not forget to relate, that to this pile of desolation, on which, like the fallen angel on the top of Niphates, we stood contemplating our nether Eden, his excellency was pleased to give the name of *Tench's Prospect Mount*.

Our fatigue to-day had been excessive: but our two sable companions seemed rather enlivened than exhausted by it. We had no sooner halted, and given them something to eat, than they began to play ten thousand tricks and gambols. They imitated the leaping of the kanguroo; sang; danced; poized the spear; and met in mock encounter. But their principal source of merriment was again derived from our misfortunes, in tumbling amidst nettles, and sliding down precipices, which they mimicked with inimitable drollery.—They had become, however, very urgent in their inquiries about the time of our return; and we pacified them as well as we could, by saying it would be soon ; but avoided naming how many days. Their method of testifying dislike to any place is singular: they point to the spot they are upon, and all around it, crying *Wee-ree, Wee-ree*, (bad) and immediately after mention the name of any other place to which they are attached, (Rose Hill or Sydney for instance) adding to it *Bud-ye-ree, Bud-ye-ree* (good). Nor was their preference in the present case the result of caprice; for they assigned very substantial reasons for such predilection : " At Rose Hill," said they, " are potatoes, cabbages, pumpkins, " turnips, fish, and wine: here are nothing but rocks and water." These comparisons constantly ended with the question of " where's Rose Hill; where?" on which they would throw up their hands, and utter a sound to denote distance, which it is impossible to convey an idea of upon paper.

Thursday, April 14th, 1791. We started early, and reached the river in about two hours and a half. The intermediate country, except for the last half mile, was a continued bed of stones, which were in some places so thick and close together, that they looked like a pavement formed by art. When we got off the stones, we came upon the coarse river sand beforementioned.

Here we began to trace upward. We had not proceeded far, when we saw several canoes on the river. Our natives made us immediately lie down among the reeds, while they gave their countrymen the signal of approach. After much calling, finding that they did not come, we continued our progress until it was again interrupted by a creek, over which we threw a tree, and passed upon it. While this was doing, a native, from his canoe, entered into conversation with us, and immediately after, paddled to us, with a frankness and confidence, which surprized every one. He was a man of middle age, with an open cheerful countenance, marked with the *small pox*, and distinguished by a nose of uncommon magnitude and dignity: he seemed to be neither astonished, or terrified at our appearance and number. Two stone hatchets, and two spears, he took from his canoe, and presented to the governor, who in return for his courteous generosity, gave him two of our hatchets, and some bread, which was new to him, for he knew not its use, but kept looking at it, until Colbee shewed him what to do, when he eat it without hesitation. We pursued our course, and to accommodate us, our new acquaintance pointed out a path, and walked at the head of us; a canoe, also with a man and a boy in it, kept gently paddling up abreast of us. We halted for the night, at our usual hour, on the bank of the river. Immediately that we had stopped, our friend (who had already told us his name)

Gom-beè-ree, introduced the man and the boy, from the canoe, to us: the former was named Yèl-lo-mun-dee, the latter Dèe-im-ba. The ease with which these people behaved among strangers, was as conspicuous, as unexpected. They seated themselves at our fire, partook of our biscuit and pork, drank from our canteens, and heard our guns going off around them, without betraying any symptom of fear, distrust, or surprize. On the opposite bank of the river, they had left their wives and several children, with whom they frequently discoursed; and we observed, that these last manifested neither suspicion, or uneasiness of our designs towards their friends.

Having refreshed ourselves, we found leisure to enter into conversation with them. It could not be expected that they should differ materially from the tribes with whom we were acquainted. The same manners and pursuits, the same amusements, the same levity and fickleness, undoubtedly characterized them. What we were able to learn from them was, that they depend but little on fish, as the river yields only mullets, and that their principal support is derived from small animals which they kill, and some roots (a species of wild yam chiefly) which they dig out of the earth. If we rightly understood them, each man possesses two wives. Whence can arise this superabundance of females? Neither of the men had suffered the extraction of a front tooth. We were eager to know whether or not, this custom obtained among them. But neither Colbee, nor Boladeree, would put the question for us; and on the contrary, shewed every desire to wave the subject. The uneasiness which they testified, whenever we renewed it, rather served to confirm a suspicion, which we had long entertained, that this is a mark of subjection imposed by the tribe of Cameragal, (who are certainly the most powerful community in the country) on the weaker tribes around them. Whether the women cut off a joint of

one of the little fingers, like those on the sea coast, we had no opportunity of observing.—These are petty remarks. But one variety
struck us more forcibly. Although our natives and the strangers
conversed on a par, and understood each other perfectly, yet they
spoke different dialects of the same language ; many of the most
common and necessary words, used in life, bearing no similitude,
and others being slightly different.

English.	Name on the sea coast.	Name at the Hawkes-bury.
The Moon	Yèn-ee-da	Con-dò-en
The Ear	Goo-reè	Bèn-na
The Forehead	Nùl-lo	Nar-ràn
The Belly	Bar-an`g	Bin`-dee
The Navel	Mùn-ee-ro	Boom-bon`g
The Buttocks	Boong	Bay-leè
The Neck	Càl-ang	Gan-gà
The Thigh	Tàr-a	Dàr-a
The Hair	Deè-war-a	Keè-war-a

That these diversities arise from want of intercourse with the
people on the coast, can hardly be imagined, as the distance inland is but thirty-eight miles ; and from Rose Hill not more than
twenty, where the dialect of the sea coast is spoken. It deserves
notice, that all the different terms seemed to be familiar to both
parties, though each in speaking preferred its own.*

* How easily people, unused to speak the same language, mistake each other, every
one knows.—We had lived almost three years at Port Jackson (for more than half of which

Stretched out at ease before our fire, all sides continued to chat and entertain each other. Gombeeree shewed us the mark of a wound which he had received in his side from a spear : it was large, appeared to have passed to a considerable depth, and must certainly have been attended with imminent danger. By whom it had been inflicted, and on what occasion, he explained to Colbee ; and afterwards (as we understood) he entered into a detail of the wars, and, as effects lead to causes, probably of the gallantries of the district ; for the word which signifies a woman, was often repeated. Colbee, in return for his communication, informed him who we were ; of our numbers at Sydney and Rose Hill ; of the stores we possessed ; and above all, of the good things which were to be found among us, enumerating potatoes, cabbages, turnips, pumpkins, and many other names which were perfectly unintelligible to the person who heard them, but which he nevertheless listened to with profound attention.

Perhaps the relation given by Gombeeree, of the cure of his wound, now gave rise to the following superstitious ceremony.

period, natives had resided with us) before we knew that the word Bèe-al, signified no, and not good, in which latter sense, we had always used it, without suspecting that we were wrong ; and even without being corrected by those with whom we talked daily.—The cause of our error was this.—The epithet Wee-ree, signifying bad, we knew ; and as the use of this word, and its opposite, afford the most simple form of denoting consent, or disapprobation, to uninstructed Indians, in order to find out their word for good, when Arabanoo was first brought among us, we used jokingly to say, that any thing, which he liked, was Weeree, in order to provoke him to tell us that it was good. When we said *Weeree*, he answered *Beeal*, which we translated, and adopted for good ; whereas he meant no more than simply to deny our inference, and say, no—it is not bad.—After this, it cannot be thought extraordinary, that the little vocabulary, inserted in Mr. Cooke's account of this part of the world, should appear defective ; even were we not to take in the great probability of the dialects at Endeavour river, and Van Deeman's land, differing from that spoken at Port Jackson. And it remains to be proved, that the amimal, called here Pat-a-ga-ram, is not there called Kanguroo.

While they were talking, Colbee turned suddenly round and asked for some water. I gave him a cup-full, which he presented with great seriousness to Yellomundee, as I supposed to drink. This last indeed took the cup, and filled his mouth with water; but instead of swallowing it, threw his head into Colbee's bosom; spit the water upon him; and immediately after, began to suck strongly at his breast, just below the nipple. I concluded that the man was sick; and called to the governor to observe the strange place which he had chosen to exonerate his stomach. The silent attention observed by the other natives, however, soon convinced us that something more than merely the accommodation of Yellomundee, was intended. The ceremony was again performed; and after having sucked the part for a considerable time, the operator pretended to receive something in his mouth, which was drawn from the breast. With this he retired a few paces, put his hand to his lips, and threw into the river a stone, which I had observed him to pick up slily, and secrete. When he returned to the fire-side, Colbee assured us, that he had received signal benefit from the operation; and that this second *Machaon*, had extracted from his breast, two splinters of a spear, by which he had been formerly wounded. We examined the part, but it was smooth and whole; so that to the force of imagination alone must be imputed both the wound and its cure. Colbee himself, seemed nevertheless firmly persuaded that he had received relief; and assured us that Yellomundee was a Cár-ad-yee, or Doctor of renown. And Boladeree added, that not only he, but all the rest of his tribe were Cár-ad-yee of especial note and skill.

The Doctors remained with us all night, sleeping before the fire in the fullness of good faith and security. The little boy slept in his father's arms; and we observed, that whenever the man was inclined to shift his position, he first put over the child, with great care, and then turned round to him.

Friday, April 15th, 1791. The return of light aroused us to the repetition of toil. Our friends breakfasted with us ; and previous to starting, Gombeeree gave a specimen of their manner of climbing trees, in quest of animals. He asked for a hatchet, and one of ours was offered to him ; but he preferred one of their own making. With this tool, he cut a small notch in the tree he intended to climb, about two feet and a half above the ground, in which he fixed the great toe of his left foot, and sprung upwards, at the same time embracing the tree with his left arm : in an instant he had cut a second notch for his right toe on the other side of the tree, into which he sprung ; and thus alternately cutting on each side, he mounted to the height of twenty feet, in nearly as short a space as if he had ascended by a ladder, although the bark of the tree, was quite smooth and slippery ; and the trunk four feet in diameter, and perfectly strait. To us it was a matter of astonishment ; but to him it was sport ; for while employed thus, he kept talking to those below, and laughing immoderately. He descended with as much ease and agility, as he had raised himself. Even our natives allowed that he was a capital performer, against whom, they dared not to enter the lists ; for as they subsist chiefly by fishing, they are less expert at climbing on the coast than those who daily practice it.

Soon after they bade us adieu, in unabated friendship and good humour. Colbee and Boladeree parted from them with a slight nod of the head, the usual salutation of the country ; and we shook them by the hand, which they returned lustily.

At the time we started, the tide was flowing up the river, a decisive proof that we were below Richmond Hill. We had continued our march but a short time when we were again stopped by a creek, which baffled all our endeavours to cross it ; and seemed to predict that the object of our attainment, though but a very few miles distant, would take us yet a considerable time to reach, which threw a damp on our hopes. We traced the creek until four o'clock, when we halted for the night. The country, on both sides, we thought in general unpromising; but it is certainly very superior to that which we had seen on the former creek. In many places it might be cultivated, provided the inundations of the stream can be repelled.

In passing along we shot some ducks, which Boladeree refused to swim for, when requested; and told us, in a surly tone, that they swam for what was killed, and had the trouble of fetching it ashore, only for the white men to eat it. This reproof was, I fear, too justly founded; for of the few ducks we had been so fortunate as to procure, little had fallen to their share, except the offals, and now and then a half-picked bone. True, indeed, all the crows and hawks which had been shot were given to them; but they plainly told us that the taste of ducks was more agreeable to their palates; and begged they might hereafter partake of them.— We observed that they were thoroughly sick of the journey, and wished heartily for its conclusion: the exclamation of " Where's Rose Hill; where?" was incessantly repeated, with many inquiries about when we should return to it.

Saturday, April 16*th,* 1791. It was this morning resolved to abandon our pursuit, and to return home; at hearing of which, our natives expressed great joy. We started early; and reached Rose Hill about three o'clock, just as a boat was about to be sent down to Sydney. Colbee and Boladeree would not wait for us until the following morning; but insisted on going down immediately, to communicate to Baneelon, and the rest of their countrymen, the novelties they had seen.

The country we passed through, was, for the most part, very indifferent, according to our universal opinion. It is in general badly watered: for eight miles and a half on one line, we did not find a drop of water.

RICHMOND HILL

Having eluded our last search, Mr. Dawes and myself, accompanied by a serjeant of marines and a private soldier, determined on another attempt, to ascertain whether it lay on the Hawkesbury or Nepean. We set out on this expedition on the 24th of May, 1791; and having reached the *opposite* side of the mouth of the creek which had in our last journey prevented our progress, we proceeded from there up to Richmond Hill, by the river side; mounted it; slept at its foot; and on the following day penetrated some miles westward or inland of it, until we were stopped by a mountainous country, which our scarcity of provisions, joined to the terror of a river at our back, whose sudden rising is almost beyond computation, hindered us from exploring. To the elevation which bounded our research, we gave the name of Knight Hill, in honour of the trusty serjeant, who had been the faithful indefatigable companion of all our travels.

This excursion completely settled the long contested point about the Hawkesbury and Nepean:—we found them to be *one river*. Without knowing it, Mr. Dawes and myself had passed Richmond Hill almost a year before (in August, 1790), and from there walked on the bank of the river, to the spot where my discovery of the Nepean happened, in June, 1789. Our ignorance arose from having never before seen the hill; and from the erroneous position assigned to it by those who had been in the boats up the river.

Except the behaviour of some natives whom we met on the river, which it would be ingratitude to pass in silence, nothing particularly worthy of notice, occurred on this expedition.

When we had reached within two miles of Richmond Hill, we heard a native call: we directly answered him, and conversed across the river for some time. At length he launched his canoe, and crossed to us without distrust or hesitation. We had never seen him before; but he appeared to know our friend Gombeeree, of whom he often spoke: he said his name was Dee-dò-ra. He presented us with two spears and a throwing-stick, and in return we gave him some bread and beef. Finding that our route lay up the river, he offered to accompany us; and getting into his canoe, paddled up abreast of us. When we arrived at Richmond Hill it became necessary to cross the river; but the question was, how this should be effected? Deedora immediately offered his canoe: we accepted of it, and Mr. Dawes and the soldier putting their clothes into it, pushed it before them, and by alternately wading and swimming, soon passed. On the opposite shore sat several natives, to whom Deedora called, by which precaution, the arrival of the strangers produced no alarm; on the contrary, they received them with every mark of benevolence. Deedora, in the mean while, sat talking with the serjeant and me. Soon after, another native, named Mo-rùn-ga, brought back the canoe; and now came our turn to cross. The serjeant (from a foolish trick which had been played upon him when he was a boy) was excessively timorous of water, and could not swim. Morunga offered to conduct him, and they got into the canoe together; but his fears returning, he jumped out and refused to proceed. I endeavoured to animate him; and Morunga ridiculed his apprehensions, making signs of the ease and dispatch with which he would land him: but he resolved to paddle over by himself, which, by dint of good management, and keeping his position very steadily, he performed. It was now become necessary to bring over the canoe a third time for my accommodation, which was instantly done, and I entered it with Deedora. But, like the serjeant, I was so disordered at seeing the water within a hair's breadth of the level of our skiff, (which brought to my remembrance a former disaster I had experienced on this river) that I jumped out, about knee-deep, and determined to swim over, which I effected. My clothes, half our knapsacks, and three of our guns, yet remained to be transported across. These I recommended to the care of our grim ferrymen, who instantaneously loaded their boat with them, and delivered them on the opposite bank, without damage or diminution.

During this long trial of their patience, and courtesy, in the latter part of which I was entirely in their power, from their having possession of our arms, they had manifested no ungenerous sign of taking advantage of the helplessness and dependance of our situation ; no rude curiosity to pry into the packages with which they were intrusted; or no sordid desire to possess the contents of them ; although among them were articles exposed to view, of which it afterwards appeared they knew the use, and longed for the benifit. Let the banks of those rivers, *"known to song ;"* let him whose travels have lain among polished nations, produce me a brighter example of disinterested urbanity, than was shewn by these denizens of a barbarous clime, to a set of destitute wanderers, on the side of the Hawkesbury.

On the top of Richmond Hill we shot a hawk, which fell in a tree. Deedora offered to climb for it, and we lent him a hatchet, the effect of which delighted him so much, that he begged for it. As it was required to chop wood for our evening fire, it could not be conveniently spared ; but we promised him, that if he would visit us on the following morning, it should be given to him. Not a murmur was heard ; no suspicion of our insincerity ; no mention

S

of benefits conferred ; no reproach of ingratitude : his good humour and cheerfulness, were not clouded for a moment. Punctual
to our appointment, he came to us at day-light next morning,
and the hatchet was given to him, the only token of gratitude and
respect in our power to bestow.—Neither of these men had lost
his *front tooth*.

THE LAST EXPEDITION

Which I ever undertook in the country I am describing, was in
July, 1791, when Mr. Dawes and myself went in search of a large
river, which was said to exist a few miles to the southward of Rose
Hill. We went to the place described, and found this second Nile,
or Ganges, to be nothing but a salt water creek, communicating
with Botany Bay, on whose banks we passed a miserable night,
from want of a drop of water to quench our thirst ; for as we believed that we were going to a river, we thought it needless to
march with full canteens.

On this expedition, we carried with us a thermometer, which (in
unison with our feelings) shewed so extraordinary a degree of cold
for the latitude of the place, that I think myself bound to trans-
scribe it.

Monday, July 18. The sun arose in unclouded splendor, and
presented to our sight a novel and picturesque view : the contiguous country as white as if covered with snow, contrasted with
the foliage of trees, flourishing in the verdure of tropical luxuriancy.* Even the exhalation which steamed from the lake beneath,

---

* All the trees of New South Wales, may, I apprehend, be termed evergreen. For after such
weather as this journal records, I did not observe either that the leaves had dropped off, or
that they had assumed that sickly autumnal tint, which marks English trees in corresponding
circumstances.

contributed to heighten the beauty of the scene.—Wind SSW.—
Thermometer at sunrise 25°.—The following night was still colder.
At sunset, the thermometer stood at 45°; at a quarter before four
in the morning, it was at 26°; at a quarter before six, at 24°; at a
quarter before seven, at 23°; at seven o'clock, 22°, 7; at sunrise,
23°; after which it continued gradually to mount, and between
one and two o'clock, stood at 59°,6, in the shade.—Wind SSW.
The horizon perfectly clear all day, not the smallest speck to be
seen.—Nothing but demonstration could have convinced me, that
so severe a degree of cold ever existed in this low latitude.
Drops of water on a tin pot, not altogether out of the influence
of the fire, were frozen into solid ice, in less than twelve minutes.
Part of a leg of kanguroo, which we had roasted for supper, was
frozen quite hard, all the juices of it being converted into ice. On
those ponds which were near the surface of the earth, the covering
of ice was very thick; but on those which were lower down, it
was found to be less so, in proportion to their depression; and
wherever the water was twelve feet below the surface (which happened to be the case close to us) it was uncongealed. It remains
to be observed, that the cold of both these nights, at Rose Hill
and Sydney, was judged to be greater than had ever before been
felt.

CHAPTER XV.

Transactions of the Colony to the End of November, 1791.

THE extreme dryness of the preceding summer has been noticed. It had operated so far in the beginning of June, that we dreaded a want of water for common consumption, most of the little reservoirs in the neighbourhood of Sydney being dried up. The small stream near the town was so nearly exhausted (being only the drain of a morass) that a ship could not have watered at it, and the Supply was preparing to sink casks in a swamp, when rain fell, and banished our apprehensions.

June, 1791. On the second instant, the name of the settlement, at the head of the harbour, Rose Hill, was changed, by order of the governor, to that of Par-ra-màt-ta, the native name of it. As Rose Hill has, however, occurred so often in this book, I beg leave, to avoid confusion, still to continue the appellation in all future mention of it.

June, 1791. Our travelling friend Boladeree, who makes so conspicuous a figure in the last chapter, about this time committed an offence which we were obliged to notice. He threw a spear at a convict in the woods, and wounded him. The truth was, some mischievous person belonging to us had wantonly destroyed his canoe, and he revenged the injury on the first of our people whom he met unarmed. He now seemed to think the matter adjusted ; and probably, such is the custom they observe in their own society in similar cases. Hearing, however, that an order was issued to seize him, or, in case that could not be effected, to shoot him, he prudently dropped all connexion with us, and was for a long time not seen.

But if they sometimes injured us, to compensate, they were often of signal benefit to those who needed their assistance ; two instances of which had recently occurred. A boat was overset in the harbour ; Baneelon, and some other natives, who saw the accident happen, immediately plunged in, and saved all the people. When they had brought them on shore, they undressed them, kindled a fire, and dried their clothes, gave them fish to eat, and conducted them to Sydney.

The other instance was of a soldier lost in the woods, when he met a party of natives : he at first knew not whether to flee from them, or to implore their assistance. Seeing among them one whom he knew, he determined to communicate his distress to him, and to rely on his generosity. The Indian told him, that he had wandered a long way from home, but that he would conduct him thither, on the single condition of his delivering up a gun which he held in his hand, promising to carry it for him, and to restore it to him at parting. The soldier felt little inclination to surrender his arms, by which he would be put entirely in their power. But seeing no alternative, he at last consented ; on which, the whole party laid down their spears, and faithfully escorted him to the nearest part of the settlement, where the gun was given up, and they took their leave without asking for any remuneration, or even seeming to expect it.

The distressful state of the colony for provisions, continued gradually to augment until the 9th of July, when the Mary Anne transport, arrived from England. This ship had sailed from the Downs, so lately as the 25th of February, having been only four months and twelve days on her passage. She brought out convicts, by contract, at a specific sum for each person. But to demonstrate the effect of humanity and justice, of one hundred and forty-four female convicts embarked on board, only three had died; and the rest were landed in perfect health, all loud in praise of their conductor. The master's name was Munro; and his ship, after fulfilling her engagement with government, was bound on the southern fishery. The reader must not conclude that I sacrifice to dull detail, when he finds such benevolent conduct minutely narrated. The advocates of humanity are not yet become too uumerous: but those who practise its divine precepts, however humble and unnoticed be their station, ought not to sink into obscurity, unrecorded and unpraised, with the vile monsters who deride misery, and fatten on calamity.

July, 1791. If, however, the good people of this ship delighted us with their benevolence, here gratification ended. I was of a party who had rowed in a boat six miles out to sea, beyond the harbour's mouth, to meet them : and what was our disappointment, on getting aboard, to find that they had not brought a letter (a few official ones for the governor excepted) to any person in the colony! Nor had they a single newspaper or magazine in their possession; nor could they conceive that any person wished to hear news ; being as ignorant of every thing which had passed in Europe for the last two years, as ourselves, at the distance of half the circle. " No " war ;—the fleet's dismantled" was the whole that we could learn. When I asked whether a new parliament had been called, they stared at me in stupid wonder, not seeming to comprehend that such a body either suffered renovation, or needed it. " Have the " French settled their government?"—" As to that matter I can't " say ; I never heard ; but, d—n them, they were ready enough " to join the Spaniards against us."—" Are Russia and Turkey at " peace?"—" That you see does not lie in my way ; I have heard

" talk about it, but don't remember what passed."—" For hea-
" ven's sake, why did you not bring out a bundle of newspapers:
" you might have procured a file at any coffee-house; which would
" have amused you, and instructed us?"—" Why, really, I never
" thought about the matter, until we were off the Cape of Good
" Hope, when we spoke a man of war, who asked us the same ques-
" tion, and then I wished I had."—To have prosecuted inquiry
farther would have only served to increase disappointment and
chagrin. We therefore quitted the ship, wondering and lamenting
that so large a portion of plain undisguised honesty should be so
totally unconnected with a common share of intelligence, and acquaintance with the feelings and habits of other men.

By the governor's letters we learned that a large fleet of transports, with convicts on board, and his Majesty's ship Gorgon, captain Parker, might soon be expected to arrive. The following intelligence which they contained, was also made public.—" That
" such convicts as had served their period of transportation, were
" not to be compelled to remain in the colony; but that no temp-
" tation should be offered to induce them to quit it; as there ex-
" isted but too much reason to believe, that they would return to
" former practices: that those who might choose to settle in the
" country, should have portions of land, subject to stipulated re-
" strictions; and a portion of provisions assigned to them, on sig-
" nifying their inclinations: and that it was expected, that those
" convicts who might be possessed of means to transport them-
" selves from the country, would leave it free of all incumbrances
" of a public nature."

July, 1791. The rest of the fleet continued to drop in, in this
and the two succeeding months. The state of the convicts whom
they brought out, though infinitely preferable to what the fleet of
last year had landed, was not unexceptionable. Three of the ships

had naval agents on board to controul them, consequently, if complaint had existed there, it would have been immediately redressed. Exclusive of these, the Salamander, captain Nichols, who, of one hundred and fifty-five men, lost only five; and the William and Anne, captain Buncker, who of one hundred and eighty-seven men lost only seven, I find most worthy of honourable mention. In the list of convicts brought out, was *Barrington*, of famous memory.

Two of these ships also added to our geographic knowledge of the country. The Atlantic, under the direction of lieutenant Bowen, a naval agent, ran into a harbour, between Van Deeman's land, and Port Jackson, in latitude 35° 12' south; longitude 151° east; to which, in honour of Sir John Jervis, knight of the bath, Mr. Bowen gave the name of Port Jervis. Here was found good anchoring ground, with a fine depth of water, within a harbour about a mile and a quarter broad, at its entrance, which afterwards opens into a bason five miles wide, and of considerable length. They found no fresh water; but as their want of this article was not urgent, they did not make sufficient researches to pronounce that none existed there.* They saw, during the short time they staid, two kanguroos, and many traces of inhabitants. The country at a little distance to the southward of the harbour is hilly; but that contiguous to the sea is flat. On comparing what they had found here afterwards, with the native produce of Port Jackson, they saw no reason to think that they differed in any respect.

The second discovery was made by captain Wetherhead, of the Matilda transport, which was obligingly described to me, as follows, by that gentleman, on my putting to him the underwritten questions.

---

* Just before I left the country, word was brought by a ship, which had put into Port Jervis, that a large fresh water brook was found there.

" When did you make your discovery ?"—" On the 27th of July,
" 1791."—"In what latitude and longitude does it lie ? —" In 42°
" 15′ south by observation, and in 148½ east by reckoning."—" Is
" it on the main land ; or is it an island ?"—" It is an island, dis-
" tant from the main land about eight miles."—Did you an-
" chor ?"—"Yes ; and found good anchorage in a bay open about
" six points."—" Did you see any other harbour or bay in the
" island ?"—" None."—" Does the channel between the island and
" the main, appear to afford good shelter for shipping ?"—" Yes ;
" like Spithead."—" Did you find any water on the island ;"—"Yes,
" in plenty."—" Of what size does the island appear to be ;"—" It
" is narrow and long ; I cannot say how long : its breadth is in-
" considerable."—" Did you make any observations on the soil ?"—
" It is sandy ; and many places are full of craggy rocks."—" Do
·" you judge the productions which you saw on the island to be
" similar to those around Port Jackson ?"—" I do not think they
" differ in any respect "—" Did you see any animals ?"—" I saw
" three kanguroos."—" Did you see any natives ; or any marks of
" them ?"—" I saw no natives ; but I saw a fire, and several huts
" like those at Port Jackson, in one of which lay a spear."—" What
" name did you give to your discovery ?"—" I called it, in honour
" of my ship, Matilda Bay."

November, 1791.   A very extraordinary instance of folly stimulated to desperation, occurred in the beginning of this month,
among the convicts at Rose Hill.   Twenty men, and a pregnant
woman, part of those who had arrived in the last fleet, suddenly
disappeared with their clothes, working tools, bedding, and their
provisions, for the ensuing week, which had been just issued to them.
The first intelligence heard of them, was from some convict settlers, who said they had seen them pass, and had enquired whither they
were bound. To which they had received for answer, " to *China.*"

T

The extravagance and infatuation of such an attempt was explained to them, by the settlers; but neither derision, nor demonstration, could avert them from pursuing their purpose. It was observed by those who brought in the account, that they had general idea enough of the point of the compass, in which China lies from Port Jackson, to keep in a northerly direction.

An officer, with a detachment of troops, was sent in pursuit of them; but after a harrassing march returned without success. In the course of a week the greatest part of them were either brought back by different parties who had fallen in with them; or were driven in by famine. Upon being questioned about the cause of their elopement, those whom hunger had forced back, did not hesitate to confess, that they had been so grossly deceived, as to believe that China might easily be reached, being not more than a hundred miles distant, and separated only by a river. The others, however, ashamed of the merriment excited at their expence, said that their reason for running away, was on account of being overworked, and harshly treated; and that they preferred a solitary and precarious existence in the woods, to a return to the misery they were compelled to undergo. One or two of the party had certainly perished by the hands of the natives; who had also wounded several others.

I trust that no man would feel more reluctant than myself, to cast an illiberal national reflection; particularly on a people whom I regard, in an aggregate sense, as brethren, and fellow-citizens; and among whom, I have the honour to number many of the most cordial and endearing intimacies, which a life passed on service could generate.—But it is certain that all these people were *Irish*.

CHAPTER XVI.

Transactions of the Colony until the 18th of December, 1791, when I quitted it; with an Account of its State at that time.

THE Gorgon had arrived on the 21st of September, and the hour of departure to England, for the marine battalion, drew nigh. If I be allowed to speak from my own feelings on the occasion, I will not say that we contemplated its approach with mingled sensations:—we hailed it with rapture and exultation.

The Supply, ever the harbinger of welcome and glad tidings, proclaimed by her own departure, that ours was at hand. On the 26th of November she sailed for England. It was impossible to view our separation with insensibility :—the little ship which had so often agitated our hopes and fears ; which from long acquaintance we had learned to regard as part of ourselves ; whose doors of hospitality had been ever thrown open to relieve our accumulated wants, and chase our solitary gloom !

December, 1791. In consequence of the offers made to the noncommissioned officers and privates of the marine battalion, to remain in the country, as settlers, or to enter into the New South Wales corps, three corporals, one drummer, and 59 privates, accepted of grants of land, to settle at Norfolk Island and Rose Hill. Of these men, several were undoubtedly possessed of sufficient skill and industry, by the assistance of the pay which was due to them from the date of their embarkation, in the beginning of the year

1787, to the day on which they were discharged, to set out with reasonable hopes of being able to procure a maintenance. But the only apparent reason to which the behaviour of a majority of them could be ascribed, was from infatuated affection to female convicts, whose characters and habits of life, I am sorry to say, promise from a connexion neither honour nor tranquillity.

The narrative part of this work will, I conceive, be best brought to a termination, by a description of the existing state of the colony, as taken by myself, a few days previous to my embarkation in the Gorgon, to sail for England.

" December 2d, 1791. Went up to Rose Hill.—Public build-
" ings here have not greatly multiplied since my last survey.
" The store-house and barrack have been long completed; also
" apartments for the chaplain of the regiment, and for the judge-
" advocate, in which last criminal courts, when necessary, are
" held; but these are petty erections. In a colony which con-
" tains only a few hundred hovels, built of twigs and mud, we
" feel consequential enough already to talk of a treasury, an
" admiralty, a public library, and many other similar edifices,
" which are to form part of a magnificent square.—The great
" road from near the landing place to the governor's house is
" finished, and a very noble one it is, being of great breadth, and
" a mile long, in a strait line: in many places it is carried over
" gullies of considerable depth, which have been filled up with
" trunks of trees, covered with earth. All the sawyers, carpenters,
" and blacksmiths will soon be concentred under the direction of
" a very adequate person of the governor's household: this plan
" is already so far advanced as to contain nine covered sawpits,
" which change of weather cannot disturb the operations of, an
" excellent work-shed for the carpenters, and a large new shop
" for the blacksmiths; it certainly promises to be of great public

" benefit: a new hospital has been talked of for the last two years,
" but is not yet begun; two long sheds, built in the form of a tent,
" and thatched, are however finished, and capable of holding two
" hundred patients ; the sick list of to-day contains three hundred
" and eighty-two names. Rose Hill is less healthy than it used to
" be ; the prevailing disorder is a dysentery, which often termi-
" nates fatally: there was lately one very violent putrid fever,
" which, by timely removal of the patient, was prevented from
" spreading : twenty-five men and two children died here in the
" month of November. When at the hospital I saw and conversed
" with some of the *Chinese travellers* ; four of them lay here,
" wounded by the natives. I asked these men if they really sup-
" posed it possible to reach China : they answered, that they were
" certainly made to believe (they knew not how) that at a consi-
" derable distance to the northward existed a large river, which se-
" parated this country from the back part of China ; and that when
" it should be crossed (which was practicable) they would find
" themselves among a copper-coloured people, who would receive
" and treat them kindly : they added, that on the third day of
" their elopement, one of the party died of fatigue ; another they
" saw butchered by the natives, who, finding them unarmed, at-
" tacked them, and put them to flight. This happened near
" Broken Bay, which harbour stopped their progress to the north-
" ward, and forced them to turn to the right hand, by which means
" they soon after found themselves on the sea shore, where they
" wandered about, in a destitute condition, picking up shell fish to
" allay hunger. Deeming the farther prosecution of their scheme
" impracticable, several of them agreed to return to Rose Hill.
" which with difficulty they accomplished, arriving almost famish-
" ed. On their road back they met six fresh adventurers, sallying
" forth to join them, to whom they related what had passed, and

" persuaded them to relinquish their intention.—There are at this
" time not less than thirty-eight convict men missing, who live in
" the woods by day, and at night enter the different farms and
" plunder for subsistence.

" December 3d, 1791. Began my survey of the cultivated land
" belonging to the public. The harvest has commenced ; they are
" reaping both wheat and barley: the field between the barrack
" and the governor's house contains wheat and maize, both very
" bad, but the former particularly so. In passing through the
" main street I was pleased to observe the gardens of the convicts
" look better than I had expected to find them. The vegetables
" in general are but mean, but the stalks of maize, with which they
" are interspersed, appear green and flourishing. The semicir-
" cular hill, which sweeps from the overseer of the cattle's house
" to the governor's house, is planted with maize, which, I am told,
" is the best here ; it certainly looks in most parts very good,
" stout thick stalks, with large spreading leaves ; but I am sur-
" prized to find it so backward ; it is at least a month later than
" that in the gardens at Sydney: behind the maize is a field of
" wheat, which looks tolerably for this part of the world ; it will
" I reckon yield about twelve bushels an acre.—Continued my
" walk, and looked at a little patch of wheat in the governor's
" garden, which was sown in drills, the ground being first mixed
" with a clay, which its discoverers pretended was marle :· what-
" ever it be, this experiment bespeaks not much in favour of its
" enriching qualities ; for the corn looks miserably, and is far
" exceeded by some neighbouring spots, on which no such advan-
" tage has been bestowed.—Went round the cresent at the bottom
" of the garden, which certainly in beauty of form and situation is
" unrivalled in New South Wales. Here are eight thousand vines
" planted, all of which in another season are expected to bear

" grapes. Besides the vines, are several small fruit trees, which
" were brought in the Gorgon from the Cape, and look lively; on
" one of them are half a dozen apples, as big as nutmegs. Although
" the soil of the crescent be poor, its aspect and circular figure, so
" advantageous. for receiving and retaining the rays of the sun,
" eminently fit it for a vineyard —Passed the rivulet, and looked
" at the corn land on its northern side; on the western side of
" Clarke's house, the wheat and maize are bad , but on the eastern
" side is a field supposed to be the best in the colony. I thought
" it of good height, and the ears well filled, but it is far from thick.
" While I was looking at it, Clarke * came up: I told him I
" thought he would reap fifteen or sixteen bushels an acre; he
" seemed to think seventeen or eighteen.—I have now inspected
" all the European corn ; a man of so little experience of these
" matters as myself, cannot speak with much confidence: perhaps
" the produce may average ten bushels an acre, or twelve at the
" outside. Allowance should, however, be made in estimating the
" quality of the soil, for the space occupied by roots of trees, for
" inadequate culture, and in some measure to want of rain; less
" have fallen than was wished; but this spring was by no means
" so dry as the last. I find that the wheat grown at Rose Hill last
" year, weighed fifty-seven pounds and a half per bushel.—My
" next visit was to the cattle, which consists of two stallions, six
" mares, and two colts ; besides sixteen cows, two cow-calfs, and one
" bull-calf, which were brought out by the Gorgon: two bulls,
" which were on board, died on the passage ; so that on the young
" gentleman just mentioned depends the stocking of the colony.

* Dod, who is mentioned in my former journal of this place, had died some months
ago. And Mr. Clarke, who was put in his room, is one of the superintendants, sent out by
government, on a salary of forty pounds per annum. He was bred to husbandry, under his
father, at Lewes in Sussex; and is, I conceive, competent to his office of principal conductor
of the agriculture of Rose Hill.

" The period of the inhabitants of New South Wales being sup-
" plied with animal food, of their own raising, is too remote for a
" prudent man to calculate. The cattle look in good condition,
" and I was surprized to hear that neither corn nor fodder is given
" to them; the enclosures in which they are confined furnish
" hardly a blade of grass at present: there are people appointed
" to tend them, who have been used to this way of life, and who
" seem to execute it very well.

" Sunday, December 4th, 1791. Divine service is now performed
" here every Sunday, either by the chaplain of the settlement, or
" the chaplain of the regiment: I went to church to-day. Several
" hundred convicts were present, the majority of whom I thought
" looked the most miserable beings in the shape of humanity, I
" ever beheld : they appeared to be worn down with fatigue.

" December, 5th. Made excursions this day to view the public
" settlements. Reached the first, which is about a mile in a north-
" west direction from the governor's house. This settlement con-
" tains, by admeasurement, one hundred and thirty-four acres, a
" part of which is planted with maize, very backward, but in
" general tolerably good, and beautifully green. Thirteen large
" huts, built in the form of a tent, are erected for the convicts who
" work here; but I could not learn the number of these last, be-
" ing unable to find a superintendant, or any person who could
" give me information : ponds of water here sufficient to supply
" a thousand persons.—Walked on to the second settlement, about
" two miles farther, through an uncleared country. Here met
" Daveney, the person who planned, and now superintends, all
" the operations carried on here. He told me that he estimated
" the quantity of cleared ground here at three hundred acres ; he
" certainly over-rates it one-third, by the judgment of every
" other person ; six weeks ago this was a forest: it has been

" cleared, and the wood nearly burnt off the ground by five
" hundred men, in the before-mentioned period, or rather in thirty
" days, for only that number have the convicts worked. He said
" it was too late to plant maize, and therefore he should sow tur-
" nips, which would help to meliorate and prepare it for next
" year.—On examining the soil, I thought it in general light,
" though in some places loamy to the touch: he means to try the
" Rose Hill *marle* upon it, with which he thinks it will incorporate
" well: I hope it will succeed better than the experiment in the
" governor's garden.—I wished to know whether he had chosen
" this ground simply from the conveniency of its situation to
" Rose Hill, and its easy form for tillage, and having water; or
" from any marks which he had thought indicated good soil. He
" said that what I had mentioned, no doubt, weighed with him;
" and that he judged the soil to be good, from the limbs of many
" of the trees growing on it being *covered with moss.*"—" Are,"
said I, " your five hundred men still complete?"—" No; this day's
" muster gave only four hundred and sixty: the rest are either
" sick, and removed to the hospital, or are run away in the woods."
" How much is each labourer's daily task?"—" Seven rods; it was
" eight; but on their representing to the governor that it was
" beyond their strength to execute, he took off one."—Thirteen
" large huts, similar to those before-mentioned, contain all the
" people here. To every hut are appointed two men, as hut-
" keepers, whose only employment is to watch the huts in work-
" ing hours, to prevent them from being robbed. This has some-
" what checked depredations, and those endless complaints of the
" convicts, that they could not work, because they had nothing to
" eat, their allowance being stolen.—The working hours at this
" season (summer) are from five o'clock in the morning until ten;
" rest from ten to two; return to work at two, and continue till

U

" sunset. This surely connot be called very severe toil : but on
" the other hand must be remembered the inadequacy of a ration
" of salt provisions, with few vegetables, and unassisted by any
" liquor but water.

" Here finished my remarks on every thing of a public nature
" at Rose Hill: but having sufficient time, I determined to visit
" all the private settlers ; to inspect their labours ; and learn from
" them their schemes, their hopes, and expectations.

" In pursuance of my resolution, I crossed the country to Pro-
" spect Hill, at the bottom of which live the following thirteen
" convicts, who have accepted allotments of ground, and are be-
" come settlers."

Men's names.	Trades.	Number of acres in each allotment.	Number of acres in cultivation.
John Silverthorne – –	Weaver –	40	$1\frac{3}{4}$
Thomas Martin – –	Do. – –	40	$1\frac{1}{2}$
John Nichols – –	Gardener –	40	2
William Butler, and his wife	Seaman –	50 ⎫	4 *
—— Lisk – –	Watchmaker	40 ⎭	
William Parish, wife, and a child – – –	Seaman –	60	$2\frac{3}{4}$
William Kilby, and his wife	Husbandman	60	$1\frac{3}{4}$
Edward Pugh, wife, and two children – – –	Carpenter –	70	$2\frac{1}{2}$
Samuel Griffith – –	Butcher –	40	$1\frac{1}{2}$
John Herbert† – –			
James Castle – –	Husbandman	40	2
Joseph Marlow ‡ – –			
John Williams, and his wife	Carpenter -	50	1

* In partnership.

† Not out of his time; but allowed to work here at his leisure hours, as he has declared his intention of settling.

‡ In a similar predicament with Herbert.

" The terms on which these allotments have been granted, are,
" That the estates shall be fully ceded for ever to all who shall con-
" tinue to cultivate for five years, or more. That they shall be
" free of all taxes for the first ten years ; but after that period to
" pay an annual quit-rent of one shilling. The penalty on non-
" performance of any of these articles is forfeiture of the estate, and
" all the labour which may have been bestowed upon it. These
" people are to receive provisions, (the same quantity as the work-
" ing convicts) clothes, and medicinal assistance, for eighteen
" months from the day on which they settled.—To clear and cul-
" tivate the land, a hatchet, a tomahawk, two hoes, a spade and a
" shovel, are given to each person, whether man or woman ; and a
" certain number of cross-cut saws among the whole. To stock
" their farms, two sow pigs were promised to each settler ; but
" they almost all say they have not yet received any, of which
" they complain loudly. They all received grain to sow and plant
" for the first year. They settled here in July and August last.
" Most of them were obliged to build their own houses ; and
" wretched hovels three-fourths of them are. Should any of them
" fall sick, the rest are bound to assist the sick person two days in
" a month, provided the sickness lasts not longer than two months;
" four days labour in each year, from every person being all that
" he is entitled to. To give protection to this settlement, a cor-
" poral and two soldiers are encamped in the centre of the farms ;
" as the natives once attacked the settlers, and burnt one of their
" houses. These guards are, however, inevitably at such a dis-
" tance from some of the farms, as to be unable to afford them
" any assistance in case of another attack.

" With all these people I conversed, and inspected their labours:
" some I found tranquil and determined to persevere, provided
" encouragement should be given : others were in a state of despon-

" dency, and predicted that they should starve, unless the period of
" 18 months, during which they are to be clothed and fed, should
" be extended to three years. Their cultivation is yet in its infancy,
" and therefore opinions should not be hastily formed of what it
" may arrive at, with moderate skill and industry. They have at
" present little in the ground besides maize, and that looks not
" very promising. Some small patches of wheat which I saw are
" miserable indeed. The greatest part of the land I think but in-
" different ; being light and stoney. Of the 13 farms 10 are unpro-
" vided with water ; and at some of them they are obliged to fetch
" this necessary article from the distance of a mile and a half.
" All the settlers complain sadly of being frequently robbed by the
" runaway convicts, who plunder them incessantly.

" December 6th. Visited the settlements to the northward of
" the rivulet. The nearest of them lies about a mile due north of
" Mr. Clarke's house. Here are only the undernamed five settlers.

Men's names.	Trades.	Number of acres in each allotment.	Number of acres in cultivation.
Thomas Brown, wife, and child – – –	– – –	60 ⎫	
William Bradbury – –	– –	30 ⎬	$3\frac{1}{2}$ *
William Mold – –	– – –	30 ⎭	
Simon Burne, and wife	Hosier – –	50	3
——— Parr, and wife –	Merchant's clerk	50	$3\frac{1}{2}$

* These three cultivate in partnership.

" These settlers are placed on the same footing, in every respect
" which concerns their tenure and the assistance to be granted to
" them, as those at Prospect Hill. Near them is water. Parr and Burne
" are men of great industry. They have both good houses, which
" they hired people to build for them. Parr told me that he had
" expended thirteen guineas on his land, which nevertheless he does
" not seem pleased with. Of the three poor fellows who work in
" partnership, one (Bradbury) is run away. This man had been
" allowed to settle, on a belief, from his own assurance, that his
" term of transportation was expired ; but it was afterwards dis-
" covered that he had been cast for life. Hereupon he grew des-
" perate, and declared he would rather perish at once, than remain
" as a convict. He disappeared a week ago, and has never since
" been heard of.—Were I compelled to settle in New South Wales,
" I should fix my residence here ; both from the appearance of the
" soil, and its proximity to Rose Hill. A corporal and two privates
" are encamped here to guard this settlement, as at Prospect."

" Proceeded to the settlement called the *Ponds,* a name which I
" suppose it derived from several ponds of water, which are near
" the farms.—Here reside the fourteen following settlers.

Men's names.	Trades.	Number of acres in each allotment.	Number of acres in cultivation.
Thomas Kelly – –	Servant – –	30	$1\frac{1}{2}$
William Hubbard, and wife	Plaisterer –	50	$2\frac{1}{4}$
Curtis Brand, and wife	Carpenter –	50	3
John Ramsay, and wife	Seaman – –	50	$3\frac{1}{2}$
William Field – –	—— – –	30	$2\frac{1}{2}$
John Richards – –	Stone-cutter –	30 ⎫	$4\frac{1}{2}$ *
John Summers – –	Husbandman –	30 ⎭	
—— Varnell – –	—— –	30	1
Anthony Rope, and wife, and two children –	Bricklayer –	70	1 †
Joseph Bishop, and wife	*None* – – –	50	$1\frac{1}{2}$
Mathew Everingham, and wife – – –	Attorney's clerk	50	2
John Anderson, and wife	——————	50	2
Edward Elliot – –	Husbandman –	30 ⎫	$2\frac{1}{4}$ ‡
Joseph Marshall –	Weaver – –	30 ⎭	

* They cultivate in partnership.

† A convict who means to settle here; and is permitted to work in his leisure hours.

‡ They cultivate in partnership.

" The Prospect Hill terms of settlement, extend to this place.
" My private remarks were not many : some spots which I passed
" over I thought desirable, particularly Ramsay's farm ; and he
" deserves a good spot, for he is a civil, sober, industrious man.
" Besides his corn land, he has a well laid out little garden, in
" which I found him and his wife busily at work. He praised her
" industry to me ; and said he did not doubt of succeeding. It is not
" often seen that sailors make good farmers ; but this man I think
" bids fair to contradict the observation. The gentleman of *no*
" *trade* (his own words to me) will, I apprehend, at the conclusion
" of the time when victualling from the store is to cease, have the
" honour of returning to drag a timber or brick cart, for his mainte-
" nance. The little miaze he has planted, is done in so slovenly
" a style, as to promise a very poor crop. He who looks forward
" to eat grapes from his own vine ; and to sit under the shade of
" his own fig-tree, must labour in every country : *here* he must
" exert more than ordinary activity. The attorney's clerk I also
" thought out of his province : I dare believe that he finds cultiva-
" ting his own land, not half so easy a task, as he formerly found
" that of stringing together volumes of tautology to encumber, or
" convey away that of his neighbour.—Hubbard's farm, and Kelly's
" also, deserve regard, from being better managed than most of the
" others.—The people here complain sadly of a destructive grub,
" which destroys the young plants of maize. Many of the settlers
" have been obliged to plant twice, nay thrice, on the same land,
" from the depredations of these reptiles.—There is the same guard
" here, as at the other settlements.

" Nothing now remains for inspection but the farms on the river
" side.

" December, 7th. Went o Scheffer's farm. I found him at
" home, conversed with him, and walked with him over all his cul-

" tivated ground. He had one hundred and forty acres granted
" to him, fourteen of which are in cultivation, twelve in maize,
" one in wheat, and one in vines and tobacco. He has besides
" twenty-three acres, on which the trees are cut down, but not
" burnt off the land.—He resigned his appointment, and began his
" farm last May ; and had at first five convicts to assist him ; he
" has now four. All his maize, except three acres, is mean. This
" he thinks may be attributed to three causes : a middling soil ;
" too dry a spring ; and from the ground not being sufficiently
" pulverized before the seed was put into it. The wheat is thin and
" poor : he does not reckon its produce at more than eight or nine
" bushels. His vines, nine hundred in number, are flourishing,
" and will, he supposes, bear fruit next year. His tobacco plants
" are not very luxuriant : to these two last articles, he means prin-
" cipally to direct his exertions. He says (and truly) that they
" will always be saleable, and profitable. On one of the boundaries
" of his land is plenty of water. A very good brick house is nearly
" completed for his use, by the governor ; and in the mean time he
" lives in a very decent one, which was built for him on his settling
" here. He is to be supplied with provisions from the public store,
" and with medical assistance for eighteen months, reckoning from
" last May. At the expiration of this period he is bound to support
" himself ; and the four convicts are to be withdrawn. But if he
" shall then, or at any future period, declare himself able to main-
" tain a moderate number of these people for their labour, they will
" be assigned to him.

" Mr. Scheffer is a man of industry and respectable character. He
" came out to this country as a superintendant of convicts, at a sa-
" lary of forty pounds per annum ; and brought with him a daugh-
" ter of twelve years old. He is by birth a Hessian, and served in
" America, in a corps of Yaghers, with the rank of lieutenant. He

X

" never was professionally, in any part of life, a farmer, but he told
" me, that his father owned a small estate on the banks of the
" Rhine, on which he resided, and that he had always been fond of
" looking at, and assisting in his labours, particularly in the vine-
" yard.   In walking along, he more than once shook his head, and
" made some mortifying observations on the soil of his present do-
" main, compared with the banks of his native stream.   He assured
" me that (exclusive of the sacrifice of his salary) he has expended
" more than forty pounds, in advancing his ground to the state in
" which I saw it. Of the probabality of success in his undertaking,
" he spoke with moderation and good sense.   Sometimes he said he
" had almost despaired, and had often balanced about relinquishing
" it ; but had as often been checked by recollecting, that hardly
" any difficulty can arise, which vigour and perseverance will not
" overcome.—I asked him what was the tenure on which he held
" his estate. He offered to shew the written document, saying, that
" it was exactly the same as Ruse's. I therefore declined to trouble
" him ; and took my leave with wishes for his success and prospe-
" rity.

" Near Mr. Scheffer's farm, is a small patch of land, cleared by
" lieutenant Townson, of the New South Wales corps, about two
" acres of which are in maize and wheat, both looking very bad.

" Proceeded to the farm of Mr. Arndell, one of the assistant
" surgeons. This gentleman has six acres in cultivation, as follows,
" rather more than four in maize, one in wheat, and the remainder
" in oats and barley ; the wheat looks tolerably good, rather thin,
" but of a good height, and the ears well filled.   His farming ser-
" vant guesses the produce will be twelve bushels,* and I do not
" think he overrates it.   The maize he guesses at thirty bushels,

---

* I have received a letter from Port Jackson, dated in April 1792, which states, that the
crop of wheat turned out fifteen bushels, and the maize rather more than forty bushels.

" which from appearances, it may yield, but not more : the oats and
" barley are not contemptible ; this ground has been turned up but
" once ; the aspect of it is nearly south, on a declivity of the river,
" or arm of the sea, on which Rose Hill stands : it was cleared of
" wood about nine months ago, and sown this year for the first
" time."

" December 8th. Went this morning to the farm of Christopher
" Magee, a convict settler, nearly opposite to that of Mr. Schef-
" fer.—The situation of this farm is very eligible, provided the
" river in floods does not inundate it, which I think doubtful. This
" man was bred to husbandry, and lived eight years in America ;
" he has no less than eight acres in cultivation, five and a half in
" maize, one in wheat, and one and a half in tobacco. From the
" wheat he does not expect more than ten bushels : but he is ex-
" travagant enough to rate the produce of maize at one hundred
" bushels ; perhaps he may get fifty ; on tobacco, he means to go
" largely hereafter. He began to clear this ground in April, but
" did not settle until last July. I asked by what means he had
" been able to accomplish so much ?" He answered, " by industry,
" and by hiring all the convicts I could get to work in their leisure
" hours, besides some little assistance which the governor has
" occasionally thrown in."—" His greatest impediment is want
" of water, being obliged to fetch all he uses, more than half
" a mile. He sunk a well, and found water, but it was brackish,
" and not fit to drink. If this man shall continue in habits of
" industry and sobriety, I think him sure of succeeding.

" Reached Ruse's farm,* and begged to look at his grant, the
" material part of which runs thus,—A lot of thirty acres, to be

* See the state of this farm in my former Rose Hill journal of November, 1790, thirteen
months before.

" called Experiment Farm ; the said lot to be holden, free of all
" taxes, quit-rents, &c. for ten years, provided that the occupier,
" his heirs or assigns, shall reside within the same, and proceed to
" the improvement thereof ; reserving, however, for the use of
" the crown, all timber now growing, or which hereafter shall
" grow, fit for naval purposes ; at the expiration of ten years, an
" annual quit-rent of one shilling shall be paid by the occupier in
" acknowledgment.——Ruse now lives in a comfortable brick
" house, built for him by the governor. He has eleven acres and a
" half in cultivation, and several more which have been cleared
" by convicts in their leisure hours, on condition of receiving the
" first year's crop. He means to cultivate little besides maize ;
" wheat is so much less productive. Of the culture of vineyards and
" tobacco, he is ignorant ; and with great good sense, he de-
" clared, that he would not quit the path he knew, for an uncer-
" tainty. His live stock consists of four breeding sows, and
" thirty fowls. He has been taking from the store (that is, has
" supplied himself with provisions) for some months past ; and
" his wife is to be taken off at Christmas, at which time, if he
" deems himself able to maintain a convict labourer, one is to be
" given to him.

" Crossed the river in a boat to Robert Webb's farm. This man
" was one of the seamen of the Sirius, and has taken, in conjunc-
" tion with his brother (also a seaman of the same ship) a grant of
" sixty acres, on the same terms as Ruse, save that the annual
" quit-rent is to commence at the expiration of five years, instead of
" ten. The brother is gone to England, to receive the wages due
" to them both for their services ; which money is to be expended
" by him, in whatever he judges will be most conducive to the
" success of their plan. Webb expects to do well ; talks as a man
" should talk who has just set out on a doubtful enterprize, which

" he is bound to pursue ; he is sanguine in hope, and looks only
" at the bright side of the prospect ; he has received great en-
" couragement, and assistance from the governor. He has five
" acres cleared, and planted with maize, which looks thriving, and
" promises to yield a decent crop. His house, and a small one ad-
" joining for pigs and poultry, were built for him by the go-
" vernor, who also gave him two sows and seven fowls, to which
" he adds a little stock of his own acquiring.

" Near Webb, is placed William Read, another seaman of the
" Sirius, on the same terms, and to whom equal encouragement
" has been granted.

" My survey of Rose Hill is now closed; I have inspected every
" piece of ground in cultivation here, both public and private, and
" have written from actual examination only.

" But before I bade adieu to Rose Hill, in all probability for the
" last time of my life, it struck me, that there yet remained one
" object of consideration not to be slighted : Barrington had been
" in the settlement between two and three months, and I had not
" seen him.

" I saw him with curiosity. He is tall, approaching to six feet,
" slender, and his gait and manner, bespeak liveliness and acti-
" vity. Of that elegance and fashion, with which my imagination
" had decked him (I know not why), I could distinguish no trace.
" Great allowance should, however, be made for depression, and
" unavoidable deficiency of dress. His face is thoughtful and in-
" telligent ; to a strong cast of countenance, he adds a penetrating
" eye, and a prominent forehead : his whole demeanour is humble,
" not servile. Both on his passage from England, and since his
" arrival here, his conduct has been irreproachable. He is ap-
" pointed high-constable of the settlement of Rose Hill, a post of
" some respectability, and certainly one of importance to those

" who live here. His knowledge of men, particularly of that part
" of them into whose morals, manners, and behaviour, he is or-
" dered especially to inspect, eminently fit him for the office.

" I cannot quit him without bearing my testimony, that his ta-
" lents promise to be directed in future, to make reparation to so-
" ciety, for the offences he has heretofore committed against it."

The number of persons, of all descriptions, at Rose Hill, at this
period, will be seen in the following return.

A return of the number of persons at Rose Hill, 3d of December, 1791.

Quality.	Men.	Women.	Children.		
			of 10 years.	of 2 years.	under 2 years.
Convicts* — —	1336	133	—	9	17
Troops — —	94	9	1	5	2
Civil Department —	7	—	—	—	—
Seamen Settlers —	3	—	—	—	—
Free Persons — —	—	7	2	1	2
Total number of persons 1628	1440	149	3	15	21

Of my Sydney journal, I find no part sufficiently interesting to
be worth extraction. This place had long been considered only as
a depôt for stores; it exhibited nothing but a few old scattered

* The convicts who are become settlers, are included in this number.

huts, and some sterile gardens: cultivation of the ground was abandoned, and all our strength transferred to Rose Hill. Sydney, nevertheless, continued to be the place of the governor's residence, and consequently the head-quarters of the colony. No public building of note, except a storehouse, had been erected, since my last statement. The barracks, so long talked of, so long promised, for the accommodation and discipline of the troops, were not even begun, when I left the country; and instead of a new hospital, the old one was patched up, and with the assistance of one, brought ready framed from England, served to contain the sick.

December, 1791. The employment of the male convicts here, as at Rose Hill, was the public labour. Of the women, the majority were compelled to make shirts, trowsers, and other necessary parts of dress, for the men, from materials delivered to them from the stores, into which they returned every Saturday night the produce of their labour, a stipulated weekly task being assigned to them. In a more early stage, government sent out all articles of cloathing ready made; but by adopting the present judicious plan, not only a public saving is effected, but employment of a suitable nature created for those who would otherwise consume leisure in idle pursuits only.

On the 26th of November, 1791, the number of persons, of all descriptions, at Sydney, was 1259, to which, if 1628, at Rose Hill, and 1172, at Norfolk Island, be added, the total number of persons in New South Wales, and its dependency, will be found to amount to 4059.*

On the 13th of December, 1791, the marine battalion embarked on board his Majesty's ship Gorgon, and on the 18th sailed for England.

* A very considerable addition to this number has been made since I quitted the settlement, by fresh troops and convicts sent thither from England.

CHAPTER. XVII.

*Miscellaneous Remarks on the Country.—On its Vegetable Productions.
On its Climate.—On its Animal Productions.—On its Natives, &c.*

THE journals contained in the body of this publication, illus-
trated by the map which accompanies it, are, I conceive, so descriptive of every part of the country known to us, that little
remains to be added beyond a few general observations.

The first impression made on a stranger is certainly favourable.
He sees gently swelling hills, connected by vales which possess
every beauty that verdure of trees, and form, simply considered in
itself, can produce: but he looks in vain for those murmuring rills
and refreshing springs, which fructify and embellish more happy
lands. Nothing like those tributary streams, which feed rivers in
other countries, are here seen: for when I speak of the stream at
Sydney, I mean only the drain of a morass; and the river at
Rose Hill is a creek of the harbour, which above high water mark
would not in England be called even a brook. Whence the
Hawkesbury, the only fresh water river known to exist in the
country, derives its supplies, would puzzle a transient observer.
He sees nothing but torpid unmeaning ponds (often stagnant and
always still, unless agitated by heavy rains) which communicate with it. Doubtless the springs which arise in Caermarthen
mountains may be said to constitute its source. To cultivate its
banks within many miles of the bed of the stream (except on

some elevated detached spots) will be found impracticable, unless some method be devised of erecting a mound, sufficient to repel the encroachments of a torrent, which sometimes rises fifty feet above its ordinary level, inundating the surrounding country in every direction.

The country between the Hawkesbury and Rose Hill, is that which I have hitherto spoken of. When the river is crossed, this prospect soon gives place to a very different one : the green vales and moderate hills disappear, at the distance of about three miles from the river side; and from Knight Hill, and Mount Twiss,* the limits which terminate our researches, nothing but precipices, wilds, and desarts, are to be seen. Even these steeps fail to produce streams. The difficulty of penetrating this country, joined to the dread of a sudden rise of the Hawkesbury, forbidding all re-return, has hitherto prevented our reaching Caermarthen mountains.

Let the reader now cast his eye on the relative situation of Port Jackson. He will see it cut off from communication with the northward by Broken Bay, and with the southward by Botany Bay; and what is worse, the whole space of intervening country yet explored (except a narrow strip called the Kanguroo ground) in both directions, is so bad as to preclude cultivation.

The course of the Hawkesbury will next attract his attention. To the southward of every part of Botany Bay we have traced this river ; but how much farther in that line it extends we know not. Hence its channel takes a northerly direction, and finishes its course in Broken Bay ; running at the back of Port Jackson, in such a manner as to form the latter into a peninsula.

The principal question then remaining is, what is the distance

* Look at the Map.

Y

between the head of Botany Bay and the part of the Hawkesbury nearest to it? And is the intermediate country a good one, or does it lead to one which appearances indicate to be good? To future adventurers, who shall meet with more encouragement to persevere and discover than I and my fellow wanderer did, I resign the answer. In the mean time the reader is desired to look at the remarks on the map, which were made in the beginning of August, 1790, from *Pyramid Hill,* which bounded our progress on the southern expedition; when, and when only, this part of the country has been seen.

It then follows, that from Rose Hill, to within such a distance of the Hawkesbury as is protected from its inundations, is the only tract of land we yet know of, in which cultivation can be carried on for many years to come. To aim at forming a computation of the distance of time, of the labour, and of the expence, which would attend forming distinct convict settlements, beyond the bounds I have delineated; or of the difficulty which would attend a system of communication between such establishments and Port Jackson, is not intended here.

Until that period shall arrive, the progress of cultivation, when it shall have once passed Prospect Hill, will probably steal along to the southward, in preference to the northward, from the superior nature of the country in that direction, as the remarks inserted in the map will testify.

Such is my statement of a plan which I deem inevitably entailed on the settlement at Port Jackson. In sketching this outline of it let it not be objected, that I suppose the reader as well acquainted with the respective names and boundaries of the country as long residence, and unweared journeying among them, have made the author. To have subjoined perpetual explanations would have been tedious and disgusting. Familiarity with the relative positions of a country can neither be imparted, or acquired, but by constant recurrence to geographic delineations.

On the policy of settling, with convicts only, a country at once so remote and extensive, I shall offer no remarks. Whenever I have heard this question agitated, since my return to England, the cry of " what can we do with them ! where else can they be sent ! has always silenced me.

Of the soil, opinions have not differed widely. A spot eminently fruitful has never been discovered. That there are many spots cursed with everlasting and unconquerable sterility no one, who has seen the country, will deny. At the same time I am decidedly of opinion, that many large tracts of land, between Rose Hill and the Hawkesbury, even now, are of a nature sufficiently favourable to produce moderate crops of whatever may be sown in them. And provided a sufficient number of cattle * be imported to afford manure for dressing the ground, no doubt can exist, that subsistence for a limited number of inhabitants, may be drawn from it. To imperfect husbandry, and dry seasons, must indubitably be attributed part of the deficiency of former years. Hitherto all our endeavours to derive advantage from mixing the different soils, have proved fruitless : though possibly only from want of skill on our side.

The spontaneous productions of the soil, will be soon recounted. Every part of the country is a forest : of the quality of the wood

---

* In my former narrative I have particularly noticed the sudden disappearance of the cattle, which we had brought with us into the country. Not a trace of them has ever since been observed. Their fate is a riddle, so difficult of solution, that I shall not attempt it. Surely had they strayed inland, in some of our numerous excursions, marks of them must have been found. It is equally impossible to believe that either the convicts, or natives, killed and eat them, without some sign of detection ensuing.

take the following instance.—The Supply wanted wood for a mast, and more than forty of the choicest young trees were cut down before as much wood as would make it could be procured : the trees being either rotten at the heart, or riven by the gum, which abounds in them. This gum runs not always in a longitudinal direction in the body of the tree, but is found in it in circles, like a scroll. There is however, a species of light wood, which is found excellent for boat building ; but it is scarce, and hardly ever found of large size. To find lime-stone many of our researches were directed. But after repeated essays with fire, and chemical preparations, on all the different sorts of stone to be picked up, it is still a *desideratum*. Nor did my experiments with a magnet induce me to think, that any of the stones I tried contained iron. I have, however, heard other people report very differently on this head. The list of esculent vegetables, and wild fruits, is too contemptible to deserve notice, if the *sweet tea*, whose virtues have been already recorded, and the common orchis root be excepted. That species of palm-tree, which produces the mountain cabbage, is also found in most of the fresh water swamps, within six or seven miles of the coast ; but is rarely seen farther inland : even the banks of the Hawkesbury are unprovided with it. The inner part of the trunk of this tree was greedily eaten by our hogs, and formed their principal support. The grass, as has been remarked in former publications, does not overspread the land in a continued sward, but arises in small detached tufts, growing every way about three inches apart, the intermediate space being bare ; though the heads of the grass are often so luxuriant, as to hide all deficiency on the surface. The rare and beautiful flowering shrubs, which abound in every part, deserve the highest admiration and panegyric.

Of the vegetable productions, transplanted from other climes, maize flourishes beyond any other grain. And as it affords a strong and nutritive article of food, its propagation will, I think, altogether supersede that of wheat and barley.

Horticulture has been attended in some places with tolerable success. At Rose Hill I have seen gardens, which, without the assistance of manure, have continued for a short time to produce well grown vegetables. But at Sydney, without constantly dressing the ground, it was in vain to expect them ; and with it a supply of common vegetables might be procured by diligence in all seasons. Vines of every sort seem to flourish : melons, cucumbers, and pumpkins, run with unbounded luxuriancy ; and I am convinced that the grapes of New South Wales will, in a few years, equal those of any other country. ‘ That their juice will probably hereafter furnish an indispensable ‘ article of luxury at European tables,’ has already been predicted in the vehemence of speculation. Other fruits are yet in their infancy ; but oranges, lemons, and figs, (of which last indeed I have eaten very good ones) will, I dare believe, in a few years become plentiful. Apples, and the fruits of colder climes, also promise to gratify expectation. The banana-tree has been introduced from Norfolk Island, where it grows spontaneously.

Nor will this surprize, if the genial influence of the climate be considered. Placed in a latitude, where the beams of the sun, in the dreariest season, are sufficiently powerful for many hours of the day to dispense warmth and nutrition, the progress of vegetation never is at a stand. The different temperatures of Rose Hill and Sydney, in winter, though only twelve miles apart, afford, however, curious matter of speculation. Of a well attested instance of ice being seen at the latter place, I never heard. At the former place, its production is common, and once a few flakes of snow fell. The difference can be accounted for, only by supposing that the woods stop the warm vapours of the sea from reaching Rose Hill, which is at the distance of sixteen miles inland ; whereas

Sydney is but four.* Again, the heats of summer are more violent at the former place, than at the latter, and the variations incomparably quicker. The thermometer has been known to alter, at Rose Hill, in the course of nine hours, more than 50°; standing a little before sunrise at 50°, and between one and two, at more than 100°. To convey an idea of the climate, in summer, I shall transcribe, from my meteorological journal, accounts of two particular days, which were the hottest we ever suffered under at Sydney.

" December 27th, 1790. Wind N N W ; it felt like the blast of " a heated oven, and in proportion as it increased, the heat was " found to be more intense, the sky hazy, the sun gleaming " through at intervals.

At 9 A. M. - - - 85°	
At noon - - - 104	
Half past twelve - - 107½	By a large Thermometer made
From one P. M. until 20 minutes past two - } 108½	by Ramsden, and graduated on Fahrenheit's scale.
At 20 minutes past two - 109	
At sunset - - - 89	
At 11 P. M. - - 78½	

December 28th.

At 8 A. M. - - 86	At a quarter past 1, it stood at
10 A. M. - - 93	only 89°, having, from a
11 A. M. - - 101	sudden shift of wind, fallen
At noon - - 103½	13° in 15 minutes.
Half an hour past noon 104½	At 5 P. M. - - - 73
At one P. M. - - 102	At sunset - - - 69½

* Look at the journal which describes the expedition in search of the river, said to exist to the southward of Rose Hill. At the time we felt that extraordinary degree of cold,

My observations on this extreme heat, succeeded by so rapid a change, were, that of all animals, man seemed to bear it best. Our dogs, pigs, and fowls, lay panting in the shade, or were rushing into the water. I remarked, that a hen belonging to me, which had sat for a fortnight, frequently quitted her eggs, and shewed great uneasiness, but never remained from them many minutes at one absence ; taught by instinct, that the wonderful power in the animal body of generating cold in air heated beyond a certain degree, was best calculated for the production of her young. The gardens suffered considerably ; all the plants, which had not taken deep root, were withered by the power of the sun. No lasting ill effects, however, arose to the human constitution ; a temporary sickness at the stomach, accompanied with lassitude and headach, attacked many, but they were removed generally in twenty-four hours by an emetic, followed by an anodyne. During the time it lasted, we invariably found, that the house was cooler than the open air, and that in proportion as the wind was excluded, was comfort augmented.

But even this heat was judged to be far exceeded in the latter end of the following February, when the north-west wind again set in, and blew with great violence for three days. At Sydney, it fell short by one degree of what I have just recorded : but at Rose Hill, it was allowed, by every person, to surpass all that they had before felt, either there, or in any other part of the world. Unluckily they had no thermometer to ascertain its precise height. It must, however, have been intense, from the effects it produced.

we were not more than six miles south west of Rose Hill, and about nineteen miles from the sea coast.—When I mentioned this circumstance to colonel Gordon, at the Cape of Good Hope, he wondered at it ; and owned, that, in his excursions into the interior parts of Africa, he had never experienced any thing to match it : he attributed its production to large beds of nitre, which he said must exist in the neighbourhood.

An immense flight of bats, driven before the wind, covered all the trees around the settlement, whence they every moment dropped dead, or in a dying state, unable longer to endure the burning state of the atmosphere. Nor did the *perroquettes*, though tropical birds, bear it better ; the ground was strewed with them in the same condition as the bats.

Were I asked the cause of this intolerable heat, I should not hesitate to pronounce, that it was occasioned by the wind blowing over immense desarts, which, I doubt not, exist in a north-west direction from Port Jackson, *and not from fires kindled by the natives*. This remark I feel necessary, as there were methods used by some persons in the colony, both for estimating the degree of heat, and for ascertaining the cause of its production, which I deem equally unfair and unphilosophical. The thermometer, whence my observations were constantly made, was hung in the open air, in a southern aspect, never reached by the rays of the sun, at the distance of several feet above the ground.

My other remarks on the climate will be short ; it is changeable beyond any other I ever heard of ; but no phænomena, sufficiently accurate to reckon upon, are found to indicate the approach of alteration. Indeed, for the first eighteen months that we lived in the country, changes were supposed to take place, more commonly at the quartering of the moon, than at other times. But lunar empire afterwards lost its credit ; for the last two years and a half of our residing at Port Jackson, its influence was unperceived. Three days together seldom passed without a necessity occuring for lighting a fire in an evening. A *habit d'ete*, or a *habit de demi sáison*, would be in the highest degree absurd ; clouds, storms, and sunshine, pass in rapid succession. Of rain, we found in general, not a sufficiency, but torrents of water sometimes fall. Thunder storms, in summer, are common, and very tremendous, but they have ceased to alarm; from rarely causing mischief; some-times they happen in winter. I have often seen large hailstones fall. Frequent strong breezes from the westward purge the air ; these are almost invariably attended with a hard clear sky. The easterly winds, by setting in from the sea, bring thick weather and rain, except in summer, when they become regular sea-breezes. The *aurora australis* is sometimes seen, but is not dis-tinguished by superior brilliancy.

To sum up :—Notwithstanding the inconveniences which I have enumerated, I will venture to assert in few words, that no climate, hitherto known, is more generally salubrious,* or affords more days, on which those pleasures, which depend on the state of the atmosphere, can be enjoyed, than that of New South Wales; the winter season is particularly delightful.

The leading animal production, is well known to be the kangu-roo. The natural history of this animal will, probably, be written from observations made upon it in England ; as several living-ones, of both sexes, have been brought home. Until such an account shall appear, probably the following desultory observa-tion may prove acceptable.

The genus in which the kanguroo is to be classed I leave to bet-ter naturalists than myself to determine.—How it copulates, those who pretend to have seen, disagree in their accounts : nor do we know how long the period of gestation lasts.—Prolific it cannot be termed, bringing forth only one at a birth, which the dam car-ries in her pouch wherever she goes, until the young one be ena-bled to provide for itself; and even then, in the moment of alarm,

---

* To this cause, I ascribe the great number of births which happened, considering the age, and other circumstances, of many of the mothers. Women, who certainly would never have bred in any other climate, here produced as fine children as ever were born.

Z

she will stop to receive and protect it. We have killed she-kan-guroos, whose pouches contained young ones, completely covered with fur, and of more than fifteen pounds weight, which had ceased to suck, and afterwards were reared by us. In what space of time it reaches such a growth, as to be abandoned entirely by the mother, we are ignorant. It is born blind, totally bald, the orifice of the ear closed, and only just the centre of the mouth open, but a black score, denoting what is hereafter to form the dimension of the mouth, is marked very distinctly on each side of the opening. At its birth, the kanguroo (notwithstanding it weighs when full grown 200 pounds) is *not so large as a half-grown mouse.* I brought some with me to England even less, which I took from the pouches of the old ones. This phenomenon is so striking, and so contrary to the general laws of nature, that an opinion has been started, that the animal is brought forth, not by the pudenda, but descends from the belly.into the pouch, by one of the teats, which are there deposited. On this difficulty, as I can throw no light, I shall hazard no conjecture. It may, however, be necessary to observe, that the teats are several inches long, and capable of great dilatation. And here I beg leave to correct an error, which crept into my former publication, wherein I asserted, that " the teats of the kanguroo, never exceed two in number." They sometimes, though rarely, amount to four. There is great reason to believe that they are slow of growth, and live many years.—This animal has a clavicle, or collar-bone, similar to that of the human body. The general colour of the kanguroo is very like that of the ass; but varieties exist: its shape and figure are well known by the plates which have been given of it.—The elegance of the ear is particularly deserving of admiration : this far exceeds the ear of the hare in quickness of sense; and is so flexible as to admit of being turned by the animal nearly quite round the head, doubtless for the purpose of informing the creature of the approach of its enemies; as it is of a timid nature, and poorly furnished with means of defence, though when compelled to resist, it tears furiously with its fore-paws, and strikes *forward* very hard with its hind legs.—Notwithstanding its unfavourable conformation for such a purpose, it swims strongly ; but never takes to the water, unless so hard pressed by its pursuers, as to be left without all other refuge. The noise they make is a faint bleat, querulous, but not easy to describe. They are sociable animals, and unite in droves, sometimes to the number of fifty or sixty together; when they are seen playful, and feeding on grass, which alone forms their food. At such time they move gently about, like all other quadrupeds, on all fours ; but at the slightest noise, they spring up on their hind legs, and sit erect, listening to what it may proceed from ; and if it increases, they bound off, on those legs only; the fore ones, at the same time, being carried close to the breast, like the paws of a monkey ; and the tail stretched out, acts as a rudder on a ship.—In drinking, the kanguroo laps.—It is remarkable that they are never found in a fat state; being invariably lean. Of the flesh we always eat with avidity ; but in Europe it would not be reckoned a delicacy: a rank flavour forms the principal objection to it.—The tail is accounted the most delicious part, when stewed.

Hitherto I have spoken only of the large, or grey kanguroo, to which the natives give the name of Pat-ag-a-ràn.* But there are (besides the kanguroo-rat) two other sorts. One of them we called the red kanguroo, from the colour of its fur, which is like that of a hare, and sometimes is mingled with a large portion of black: the natives call it Bàg-a-ray. It rarely attains to more than

---

* Kanguroo, was a name unknown to them for any animal, until we introduced it. When I shewed Colbee the cows brought out in the Gorgon, he asked me if they were kanguroos?

forty pounds weight. The third sort is very rare, and in the formation of its head, resembles the oppossum.—The kanguroo-rat is a small animal, never reaching, at its utmost growth, more than fourteen or fifteen pounds, and its usual size is not above seven or eight pounds. It joins to the head and bristles of a rat, the leading distinctions of a kanguroo, by running, when pursued, on its hind legs only, and the female having a pouch. Unlike the kanguroo, who appears to have no fixed place of residence, this little animal constructs for itself a nest of grass, on the ground, of a circular figure, about ten inches in diameter, with a hole on one side, for the creature to enter at; the inside being lined with a finer sort of grass, very soft and downy. But its manner of carrying the materials, with which it builds the nest, is the greatest curiosity:— by entwining its tail (which, like that of all the kanguroo tribe, is long, flexible, and muscular) around whatever it wants to remove, and thus dragging along the load behind it. This animal is good to eat; but whether it be more prolific at a birth than the kanguroo, I know not.

The Indians sometimes kill the kanguroo; but their greatest destroyer is the wild dog, * who feeds on them. Immediately on hearing, or seeing, this formidable enemy, the kanguroo flies to the thickest cover, in which, if he can involve himself, he generally escapes. In running to the cover, they always, if possible, keep in paths of their own forming, to avoid the high grass, and stumps of trees, which might be sticking up among it, to wound them, and impede their course.

---

* I once found in the woods the greatest part of a kanguroo, just killed by the dogs, which afforded to three of us a most welcome repast. Marks of its turns and struggles on the ground were very visible. This happened in the evening, and the dogs probably had seen us approach, and had run away —At daylight next morning they saluted us with most dreadful howling for the loss of their prey.

Our methods of killing them were but two ; either we shot them, or hunted them with greyhounds ; we were never able to ensnare them. Those sportsmen who relied on the gun, seldom met with success, unless they slept near covers, into which the kanguroos were wont to retire at night, and watched with great caution and vigilance when the game, in the morning, sallied forth to feed. They were, however, sometimes stolen in upon in the day-time ; and that fascination of the eye, which has been by some authors so much insisted upon, so far acts on the kanguroo, that if he fix his eye upon any one, and no other object move at the same time, he will often continue motionless, in stupid gaze, while the sportsman advances, with measured step, towards him, until within reach of his gun. The greyhounds for a long time were incapable of taking them ; but with a brace of dogs, if not near cover, a kanguroo almost always falls, since the greyhounds have acquired by practice the proper method of fastening upon them. Nevertheless the dogs are often miserably torn by them. The rough wiry greyhound suffers least in the conflict, and is most prized by the hunters.

Other quadrupeds, besides the wild dog, consist only of the fly-ing squirrel, of three kinds of oppossums, and some minute animals, usually marked by the distinction which so peculiarly characte-rizes the oppossum tribe. The rats, soon after our landing, became not only numerous but formidable, from the destruction they oc-casioned in the stores. Latterly they had almost disappeared, though to account for their absence were not easy.—The first time Colbee saw a monkey, he called *Wur-ra* (a rat) ; but on ex-amining its paws, he exclaimed, with astonishment and affright, *Mul-la* (a man).

At the head of the birds the cassowary, or emu, stands conspicu-ous. The print of it, which has already been given to the public, is so accurate, for the most part, that it would be malignant criticism, in a work of this kind, to point out a few trifling defects.

Here again naturalists must look forward to that information, which longer and more intimate knowledge of the feathered tribe than I can supply, shall appear. I have nevertheless had the good fortune to see what was never seen but once, in the country I am describing, by Europeans—a hatch, or flock, of young cassowaries, with the old bird. I counted ten, but others said there were twelve. We came suddenly upon them, and they ran up a hill, exactly like a flock of turkies, but so fast that we could not get a shot at them. The largest cassowary ever killed in the settlement, weighed ninety-four pounds: three young ones, which had been by accident separated from the dam, were once taken, and presented to the governor. They were not larger than so many pullets, although at first sight they appeared to be so, from the length of their necks and legs. They were very beautifully striped, and from their tender state, were judged to be not more than three or four days old. They lived only a few days.

A single egg, the production of a cassowary, was picked up in a desart place, dropped on the sand, without covering or protection of any kind. Its form was nearly a perfect ellipsis; and the colour of the shell a dark green, full of little indents on its surface. It measured eleven inches and a half in circumference, five inches and a quarter in height, and weighed a pound and a quarter.—Afterwards we had the good fortune to take a nest: it was found by a soldier, in a sequestered solitary situation, made in a patch of lofty fern, about three feet in diameter, rather of an oblong shape, and composed of dry leaves and tops of fern stalks, very inartificially put together. The hollow in which lay the eggs, twelve in number, seemed made solely by the pressure of the bird. The eggs were regularly placed in the following position.

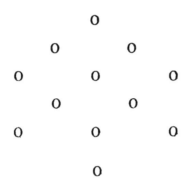

The soldier, instead of greedily plundering his prize, communicated the discovery to an officer, who immediately set out for the spot. When they had arrived there, they continued for a long time to search in vain for their object ; and the soldier was just about to be stigmatized with ignorance, credulity, or imposture, when suddenly up started the old bird, and the treasure was found at their feet.

The food of the cassowary is either grass, or a yellow bell-flower growing in the swamps.—It deserves remark, that the natives deny the cassowary to be a bird, because it does not fly.

Of other birds the varieties are very numerous. Of the parrot tribe alone I could, while I am writing, count up from memory fourteen different sorts : hawks are very numerous ; so are quails. A single snipe has been shot : ducks, geese, and other aquatic birds, are often seen in large flocks ; but are universally so shy, that it is found difficult to shoot them. Some of the smaller birds are very beautiful, but they are not remarkable for either sweetness, or variety of notes. To one of them, not bigger than a tomtit, we have given the name of coach-whip, from its note exactly resembling the smack of a whip. The country, I am of opinion, would abound with birds, did not the natives, by perpetually setting fire to the grass and bushes, destroy the greater part of the nests; a cause which also contributes to render small quadrupeds scarce : they are besides ravenously fond of eggs, and eat them wherever they find them.—They call the roe of a fish and a bird's egg by one name.

So much has been said of the abundance in which fish are found in the harbours of New South Wales, that it looks like detraction to oppose a contradiction. Some share of knowledge may, however, be supposed to belong to experience. Many a night have I toiled (in the times of distress) on the public service, from four o'clock in the afternoon, until eight o'clock next morning, hauling the seine in every part of the harbour of Port Jackson : and after a circuit of many miles, and between twenty and thirty hauls, seldom more than a hundred pounds of fish were taken. However, it sometimes happens that a glut enters the harbour, and for a few days they sufficiently abound : but the universal voice of all professed fishermen is, that they never fished in a country where success was so precarious and uncertain.

I shall not pretend to enumerate the variety of fish which are found ; they are seen from a whale to a gudgeon : in the intermediate classes may be reckoned sharks of a monstrous size, skait, rock-cod, grey-mullet, bream, horse-mackarel, now and then a sole and john-dory, and innumerable others unknown in Europe, many of which are extremely delicious, and many highly beautiful. At the top of the list, as an article of food, stands a fish, which we named light-horseman. The relish of this excellent fish was increased by our natives, who pointed out to us its delicacies. No epicure in England could pick a head with more glee and dexterity than they do that of a light-horseman.

Reptiles in the swamps and covers are numerous. Of snakes there are two or three sorts : but whether the bite of any of them be mortal, or even venomous, is somewhat doubtful: I know but of one well attested instance of a bite being received from a snake. A soldier was bitten so as to draw blood; and the wound healed as a simple incision usually does, without shewing any symptom of malignity.—A dog was *reported* to be bitten by a snake, and the animal swelled and died in great agony. But I will by no means affirm that the cause of his death was fairly ascertained. It is, however, certain, that the natives shew, on all occasions, the utmost horror of the snake, and will not eat it, although they esteem lizards, guanas, and many other reptiles, delicious fare. Or this occasion they always observe, that if the snake bites them, they become lame: but whether by this they mean temporary or lasting lameness, I do not pretend to determine.—I have often eaten snakes, and always found them palatable and nutritive, though it was difficult to stew them to a tender state.

Summer here, as in all other countries, brings with it a long list of insects. In the neighbourhood of rivers, and morasses, musquitoes and sand-flies are never wanting at any season; but at Sydney, they are seldom numerous, or troublesome. The most nauseous, and destructive of all the insects, is a fly, which blows not eggs, but large living maggots; and if the body of the fly be opened it is found full of them. Of ants, there are several sorts, one of which bites very severely: the white ant is sometimes seen. Spiders are large and numerous. Their webs are not only the strongest, but the finest, and most silky, I ever felt. I have often thought their labour might be turned to advantage. It has, I believe, been proved, that spiders, were it not for their quarrelsome disposition, which irritates them to attack and destroy each other, might be employed more profitably than silk-worms.

The hardiness of some of the insects, deserves to be mentioned. A beetle was immersed, in proof spirits, for four hours, and when

A a

taken out, crawled away almost immediately. It was a second time immersed, and continued in a glass of rum for a day and a night, at the expiration of which period, it still shewed symptoms of life. Perhaps, however, what I from ignorance deem wonderful, is common.

———————

The last, but the most important production yet remains to be considered. Whether plodding in London ; reeking with human blood in Paris; or wandering amidst the solitary wilds of New South Wales—Man is ever an object of interest, curiosity, and reflection.

The natives around Port Jackson, are in person, rather more diminitive, and slighter made, especially about the thighs and legs, than the Europeans. It is doubtful whether their society contained a person of six feet high. The tallest I ever measured, reached five feet eleven inches ; and men of his height were rarely seen. Baneelon, who towered above the majority of his countrymen, stood barely five feet eight inches high ; his other principal dimensions were as follows :—

Girth of the Chest.	Girth of the Belly.	Girth of the Thigh	Girth of the Leg at the Calf.	Girth of the Leg at the small.	Girth of the arm half way between the shoulder and elbow.
feet inches	feet inches	inches.	inches	inches	inches
2 10	2 $6\frac{1}{2}$	$18\frac{1}{8}$	$12\frac{3}{8}$	10	9

Instances of natural deformity are scarce ; nor did we ever see one of them left-handed. They are, indeed, nearly ambidexter ; but the sword, the spear, and the fish-gig, are always used with the right-hand. Their muscular force is not great ; but the pliancy of their limbs, renders them very active. " Give to civilized man all " his machines, and he is superior to the savage; but without " these, how inferior is he found on opposition, even more so than " the savage in the first instance." These are the words of Rousseau; and like many more of his positions, must be received with limitation. Were an unarmed Englishman, and an unarmed New Hollander, to engage, the latter, I think, would fall.

Mr. Cook seems inclined to believe the covering of their heads to be wool. But this is erroneous; it is certainly hair, which, when regularly combed, becomes soon nearly as flexible and docile as our own. Their teeth are not so white and good, as those generally found in Indian nations, except in the children : but the inferiority originates in themselves; they bite sticks, stones, shells, and all other hard substances, indiscriminately with them, which quickly destroys the enamel, and gives them a jagged and uneven appearance. A high forehead, with prominent overhanging eyebrows, is their leading characteristic, and when it does not operate, to destroy all openness of countenance, gives an air of resolute dignity to the aspect, which recommends, in spite of a true negro nose, thick lips, and a wide mouth. The prominent shin bone, so invariably found in the Africans, is not, however, seen. But in another particular, they are more alike; the rank offensive smell, which disgusts so much in the negro, prevails strongly among them, when they are in their native state ; but it wears off in those who have resided with us, and have been taught habits of cleanliness. Their hands and feet are small,* especially the former.

---

* I mentioned this, among other circumstances, to colonel Gordon, when I was at the Cape, and he told me, that it indicated poverty, and inadequacy of living. He instanced to me the Hottentots and Caffres; the former fare poorly, and have small hands and feet; the Caffres, their neighbours, live plenteously, and have very large ones.—This remark cannot be applied to civilized nations, where so many factitious causes operate.

Their eyes are full, black, and piercing; but the almost perpetual strain, in which the optic nerve is kept, by looking out for prey, renders their sight weak, at an earlier age, than we in general find ours affected. These large black eyes, are universally shaded by the long thick sweepy eyelash, so much prized in appreciating beauty, that, perhaps, hardly any face is so homely, which this aid cannot, in some degree, render interesting; and hardly any so lovely, which, without it, bears not some trace of insipidity. Their tone of voice is loud, but not harsh: I have, in some of them, found it very pleasing.

Longevity, I think, is seldom attained by them. Unceasing agitation wears out the animal frame, and is unfriendly to length of days. We have seen them grey with age, but not old; perhaps never beyond sixty years. But it may be said, the American Indian, in his undebauched state, lives to an advanced period. True; but he has his seasons of repose: he reaps his little harvest of maize, and continues in idleness while it lasts; he kills the roebuck, or the moose-deer, which maintains him and his family for many days, during which cessation the muscles regain their spring, and fit him for fresh toils. Whereas, every sun awakes the native of New South Wales (unless a whale be thrown upon the coast) to a renewal of labour, to provide subsistence for the present day.

The women are proportionally smaller than the men. I never measured but two of them, who were both, I think, about the medium height. One of them, a sister of Baneelon, stood exactly five feet two inches high: the other, named Goo-ree-dee-à-na, was shorter by a quarter of an inch.

But I cannot break from Gooreedeeana so abruptly.—She belonged to the tribe of Cameragal, and rarely came among us. One day, however, she entered my house, to complain of hunger. She excelled in beauty all their females I ever saw: her age about eighteen : the firmness, the symmetry, and the luxuriancy of her bosom, might have tempted painting to copy its charms : her mouth was small ; and her teeth, though exposed to all the destructive purposes to which they apply them, were white, sound, and unbroken.—Her countenance, though marked by some of the characteristics of her native land, was distinguished by a softness and sensibility, unequalled in the rest of her countrywomen : and I was willing to believe, that these traits indicated the disposition of her mind. I had never before seen this elegant timid female, of whom I had often heard ; but the interest I took in her, led me to question her about her husband and family. She answered me by repeating a name, which I have now forgotten ; and told me she had no children. I was seized with a strong propensity to learn whether the attractions of Gooreedeeana, were sufficiently powerful to secure her from the brutal violence, with which the women are treated : and as I found my question either ill understood, or reluctantly answered, I proceeded to examine her head, the part on which the husband's vengeance generally alights.—With grief I found it covered by contusions, and mangled by scars. The poor creature, grown by this time more confident, from perceiving that I pitied her, pointed out a wound just above her left knee, which she told me was received from a spear, thrown at her by a man, who had lately dragged her by force from her home, to gratify his lust. I afterwards observed, that this wound had caused a slight lameness, and that she limped in walking. I could only compassionate her wrongs, and sympathize in her misfortunes : to alleviate her present sense of them, when she took her leave, I gave her, however, all the bread and salt pork which my little stock afforded.

After this I never saw her but once, when I happened to be near the harbour's mouth, in a boat, with captain Ball. We met her in a canoe, with several more of her sex. She was painted for a ball, with broad stripes of white earth, from head to foot; so that she no longer looked like the same Gooreedeeana. We offered her several presents, all of which she readily accepted; but finding our eagerness and solicitude to inspect her, she managed her canoe with such address, as to elude our too near approach, and acted the coquet to admiration.

To return from this digression to my subject, I have only farther to observe, that the estimation of female beauty among the natives (the men at least,) is in this country the same as in most others. Were a New-Hollander to pourtray his mistress, he would draw her the *Venus aux belles fesses*. Whenever Baneelon described to us his favourite fair, he always painted her in this, and another, particular, as eminently luxuriant.

Unsatisfied, however, with natural beauty, like the people of all other countries, they strive by adscititious embellishments to heighten attraction, and often with as little success. Hence the naked savage of New South Wales, pierces the septum of his nose, through which he runs a stick or a bone; and scarifies his body, the charms of which increase in proportion to the number and magnitude of seams, by which it is distinguished. The operation is performed by making two longitudinal incisions, with a sharpened shell, and afterwards pinching up with the nails the intermediate space of skin and flesh, which thereby becomes considerably elevated, and forms a prominence as thick as a man's finger. No doubt but pain must be severely felt, until the wound be healed. But the love of ornament defies weaker considerations: and no English beau can bear more stoutly the extraction of his teeth, to make room for a fresh set from a chimney sweeper; or a fair one suffer her tender ears to be perforated, with more heroism, than the grisly nymphs, on the banks of Port Jackson, submit their sable shoulders to the remorseless lancet.

That these scarifications are intended solely to encrease personal allurement, I will not, however, positively affirm. Similar, perhaps, to the cause of an excision of part of the little finger of the left hand, in the women, and of a front tooth in the men ;* or probably after all our conjectures, superstitious ceremonies, by which they hope either to avert evil, or to propagate good, are intended. The colours with which they besmear the bodies of both sexes, possibly date from the same common origin. White paint is strictly appropriate to the dance. Red seems to be used on numberless occasions, and is considered as a colour of less consequence. It may be remarked, that they translate the epithet white, when they speak of us, not by the name which they assign to this white earth ; but by that with which they distinguish the palms of their hands.

As this leads to an important subject, I shall at once discuss it.— " Have these people any religion : any knowledge of, or believe in

---

* It is to be observed, that neither of these ceremonies is universal, but nearly so. Why there should exist exemptions I cannot resolve. The manner of executing them is as follows.— The finger is taken off by means of a ligature (generally a sinew of a kanguroo) tied so tight as to stop the circulation of the blood, which induces mortification, and the part drops off. I remember to have seen Colbee's child, when about a month old, on whom this operation had been just performed, by her mother. The little wretch seemed in pain, and her hand was greatly swelled. But this was deemed too trifling a consideration, to deserve regard, in a case of so much importance.

The tooth intended to be taken out is loosened, by the gum being scarified on both sides with a sharp shell. The end of a stick is then applied to the tooth, which is struck gently, several times, with a stone, until it becomes easily moveable, when the *coup de grace* is given,_ by a smart stroke. Notwithstanding these precautions, I have seen a considerable degree of swelling and inflammation, follow the extraction. Imeerawanyee, I remember, suffered severely. But he boasted the firmness and hardidood, with which he had endured it. It is seldom performed on those who are under sixteen years old.

" a deity?—any conception of the immortality of the soul?" are questions which have been often put to me since my arrival in England: I shall endeavour to answer them with candour and seriousness.

Until belief be enlightened by revelation, and chastened by reason; religion and superstition, are terms of equal import. One of our earliest impressions, is the consciousness of a superior power. The various forms under which this impression has manifested itself, are objects of the most curious speculation.

The native of New South Wales believes, that particular aspects and appearances of the heavenly bodies, predict good or evil consequences to himself and his friends. He oftentimes calls the sun and moon ' *weeree*,' that is, malignant, pernicious. Should he see the leading fixed stars (many of which he can call by name) obscured by vapours, he sometimes disregards the omen; and sometimes draws from it the most dreary conclusions.—I remember Abaroo running into a room, where a company was assembled, and uttering frightful exclamations of impending mischiefs, about to light on her and her countrymen. When questioned on the cause of such agitation, she went to the door, and pointed to the skies, saying, that whenever the stars wore that appearance, misfortunes to the natives always followed. The night was cloudy, and the air disturbed by meteors —I have heard many more of them testify similar apprehensions.

However involved in darkness, and disfigured by error, such a belief be, no one will, I presume, deny, that it conveys a direct implication of superior agency; of a power independent of, and uncontrolled by, those who are the objects of its vengeance:—but proof stops not here:—when they hear the thunder roll, and view the livid glare, they flee them not; but rush out and deprecate destruction. They have a dance and a song appropriated to this awful occasion, which consist of the wildest and most uncouth noises and gestures.—Would they act such a ceremony did they not conceive, that either the thunder itself, or he who directs the thunder, might be propitiated by its performance? that a living intellectual principle exists, capable of comprehending their petition, and of either granting or denying it? They never address prayers to bodies which they know to be inanimate, either to implore their protection, or avert their wrath. When the gum-tree in a tempest nods over them; or the rock overhanging the cavern in which they sleep, threatens by its fall to crush them, they calculate (as far as their knowledge extends) on physical principles, like other men, the nearness and magnitude of the danger, and flee it accordingly. And yet there is reason to believe, that from accidents of this nature they suffer more, than from lightning. Baneelon once shewed us a cave, the top of which had fallen in, and buried under its ruins seven people, who were sleeping under it.

To descend; is not even the ridiculous superstition of Colbee related in one of our journies to the Hawkesbury? And again the following instance:—Abaroo was sick; to cure her, one of her own sex slightly cut her on the forehead, in a perpendicular direction, with an oyster shell, so as just to fetch blood : she then put one end of a string to the wound, and, beginning to sing, held the other end to her own gums, which she rubbed until they bled copiously. This blood she contended was the blood of the patient, flowing though the string, and that she would thereby soon recover. Abaroo became well; and firmly believed that she owed her cure to the treatment she had received.—Are not these, I say, links, subordinate ones indeed, of the same golden chain? He who believes in magic, confesses surpernatural agency : and a belief of this sort extends farther in many persons than they are willing to allow. There have lived men so inconsistent with their own principles as to deny the existence of a God, who have nevertheless turned pale at the tricks of a mountebank.

But not to multiply arguments on a subject, where demonstration (at least to me) is incontestable, I shall close by expressing my firm belief, that the Indians of New South Wales acknowledge the existence of a superintending deity. Of their ideas of the origin and duration of his existence ; of his power and capacity ; of his benignity or maleficence ; or of their own emanation from him, I pretend not to speak. I have often, in common with others, tried to gain information from them on this head ; but we were always repulsed by obstacles, which we could neither pass by, or surmount. Mr Dawes attempted to teach Abaroo some of our notions of religion, and hoped that she would thereby be induced to communicate hers in return. But her levity, and love of play, in a great measure defeated his efforts; although every thing he did learn from her, served to confirm what is here advanced. It may be remarked, that when they attended at church with us (which was a common practice) they always preserved profound silence and decency, as if conscious that some religious ceremony on our side was performing.

The question of, whether they believe in the immortality of the soul, will take up very little time to answer. They are universally fearful of spirits.* They call a spirit, *Mawn*: they often scruple to approach a corpse, saying that the *mawn* will seize them, and that it fastens upon them in the night when asleep. † When asked where their deceased friends are, they always point to the skies. To believe in after existence is to confess the immortality of some

* " It is remarkable," says Cicero, " that there is no nation, whether barbarous or civilized, that does not believe in the existence of spirits."

† As they often eat to satiety, even to produce sickness; may not this be the effect of an overloaded stomach: the night mare.

part of being. To enquire whether they assign a *limited* period to such future state would be superfluous : this is one of the subtleties of speculation, which a savage may be supposed not to have considered, without impeachment either of his sagacity or happiness.

Their manner of interring the dead has been amply described. It is certain that instead of burying they sometimes burn the corpse ; but the cause of distinction we know not. A dead body, covered by a canoe, at whose side a sword and shield were placed in state, was once discovered. All that we could learn about this important personage was, that he was a *Gwee-a-gal*, (one of the tribe of Gweea) and a celebrated warrior.

To appreciate their general powers of mind is difficult. Ignorance, prejudice, the force of habit, continually interfere to prevent dispassionate judgment. I have heard men so unreasonable, as to exclaim at the stupidity of these people, for not comprehending what a small share of reflection would have taught them they ought not to have expected. And others again I have heard so sanguine in their admiration, as to extol for proofs of elevated genius what the commonest abilities were capable of executing.

If they be considered as a nation, whose general advancement and acquisitions are to be weighed, they certainly rank very low, even in the scale of savages. They may perhaps dispute the right of precedency with the Hottentots, or the shivering tribes who inhabit the shores of Magellan. But how inferior do they show when compared with the subtle African ; the patient watchful American ; or the elegant timid islander of the South Seas. Though suffering from the vicissitudes of their climate,—strangers to cloathing: tho' feeling the sharpness of hunger, and knowing the precariousness of supply from that element on whose stores they principally depend, ignorant of cultivating the earth,—a less enlightened state we shall exclaim can hardly exist.

But if from general view we descend to particular inspection, and examine individually the persons who compose this community, they will certainly rise in estimation. In the narrative part of this work, I have endeavoured rather to detail information, than to deduce conclusions ; leaving to the reader the exercise of his own judgment. The behaviour of Arabanoo, of Baneelon, of Colbee, and many others, is copiously described ; and assuredly he who shall make just allowance for uninstructed nature, will hardly accuse any of those persons of stupidity, or deficiency of apprehension.

To offer my own opinion on the subject, I do not hesitate to declare, that the natives of New South Wales possess a considerable portion of that acumen, or sharpness of intellect, which bespeaks genius. All savages hate toil, and place happiness in inaction : and neither the arts of civilized life can be practised, or the advantages of it felt, without application and labour. Hence they resist knowledge, and the adoption of manners and customs, differing from their own. The progress of reason is not only slow, but mechanical.—" *De toutes les instructions propres à l'homme, celle* " *qu'il acquiert le plus tard, et le plus difficilement, est la raison* " *même.*" The tranquil indifference, and uninquiring eye, with which they surveyed our works of art, have often, in my hearing, been stigmatized as proofs of stupidity, and want of reflection. But surely we should discriminate between ignorance and defect of understanding. The truth was, they often neither comprehended the design, nor conceived the utility of such works : but on subjects in any degree familiarized to their ideas, they generally testified not only acuteness of discernment, but a large portion of good sense. I have always thought that the distinctions they shewed in their estimate of us, on first entering into our society, strongly displayed the latter quality :—when they were led into our respective houses, at once to be astonished and awed by our superiority, their attention was directly turned to objects with which they were acquainted. They passed without rapture or emotion, our numerous artifices and contrivances: but when they saw a collection of weapons of war, or of the skins of animals and birds, they never failed to exclaim, and to confer with each other on the subject. The master of that house became the object of their regard, as they concluded he must be either a renowned warrior, or an expert hunter. Our surgeons grew into their esteem from a like cause. In a very early stage of intercourse, several natives were present at the amputation of a leg: when they first penetrated the intention of the operator, they were confounded; not believing it possible that such an operation could be performed without loss of life; and they called aloud to him to desist: but when they saw the torrent of blood stopped, the vessels taken up, and the stump dressed, their horror and alarm yielded to astonishment and admiration, which they expressed by the loudest tokens.—If these instances bespeak not nature and good sense, I have yet to learn the meaning of the terms.

If it be asked why the same intelligent spirit which led them to contemplate and applaud the success of the sportsman, and the skill of the surgeon, did not equally excite them to meditate on the labours of the builder, and the ploughman; I can only answer, that what we see in its remote cause, is always more feebly felt, than that which presents to our immediate grasp, both its origin and effect.

Their leading good and bad qualities I shall concisely touch upon.—Of their intrepidity no doubt can exist: their levity, their fickleness, their passionate extravagance of character, cannot be defended. They are indeed sudden and quick in quarrel; but if their resentment be, easily roused, their thirst of revenge is not im-

placable.—Their honesty, when tempted by novelty, is not unim-
peachable; but in their own society, there is good reason to believe, that few breaches of it occur.—It were well if similar praise
could be given to their veracity: but truth they neither prize nor
practice. When they wish to deceive, they scruple not to utter the
grossest and most hardened lies. *   Their attachment and gratitude to those among us, whom they have professed to love, have
always remained inviolable, unless effaced by resentment, from
sudden provocation: then, like all other Indians, the impulse of
the moment is alone regarded by them.

Some of their manufactures display ingenuity, when the rude
tools with which they work, and their celerity of execution, are
considered.—The canoes, fish-gigs, swords, shields, spears, throw-
ing-sticks, clubs, and hatchets, are made by the men: to the women are committed the fishing-lines, hooks, and nets.—As very
ample collections of all these articles are to be found in many mu-
seums in England, I shall only briefly describe the way in which
the most remarkable of them are made.—The fish-gigs and spears
are commonly (but not universally) made of the long spiral shoot,
which arises from the top of the yellow gum-tree, and bears the
flower: the former have several prongs, barbed with the bone of
kanguroo; the latter are sometimes barbed with the same substance; or with the prickle of the sting-ray; or with stone; or
hardened gum; and sometimes simply pointed.   Dexterity in
throwing, and parrying the spear, is considered as the highest ac-
quirement: the children of both sexes practice from the time that
they are able to throw a rush; their first essay.—It forms their
constant recreation.   They afterwards heave at each other with
pointed twigs. He who acts on the defensive, holds a piece of new
soft bark in the left hand, to represent a shield, in which he re-

* This may serve to account for the contradictions of many of their accounts to us.

ceives the darts of the assailant, the points sticking in it. Now
commences his turn: he extracts the twigs, and darts them back
at the first thrower, who catches them similarly —In warding off
the spear, they never present their front, but always turn their
side; their head, at the same time, just clear of the shield, to watch
the flight of the weapon; and the body covered. If a spear drop
from them, when thus engaged, they do not stoop to pick it up;
but hook it between the toes, and so lift it until it meet the hand:
thus the eye is never diverted from its object, the foe. If they wish
to break a spear, or any wooden substance, they lay it, not across
the thigh or the body, but upon the head, and press down the ends
until it snap. Their shields are of two sorts: that called *Il-ee-mon*,
is nothing but a piece of bark, with a handle fixed in the inside of
it: the other, dug out of solid wood, is ralled *Ar-a-goòn*, and is
made as follows, with great labour. On the bark of a tree, they
mark the size of the shield; then dig the outline as deep as possible in the wood, with hatchets; and lastly, flake it off as thick
as they can, by driving in wedges.—The sword is a large heavy
piece of wood, shaped like a sabre, and capable of inflicting a mortal wound: in using it, they do not strike with the convex side,
but with the concave one; and strive to hook in their antagonists,
so as to have them under their blows.—The fishing-lines are made
of the bark of a shrub: the women roll shreds of this on the inside
of the thigh, so as to twist it together, carefully inserting the ends
of every fresh piece into the last made:—they are not as strong as
lines of equal size, formed of hemp.—The fish-hooks are chopped
with a stone out of a particular shell, and afterwards rubbed until
they become smooth. They are very much curved, and not barbed.
Considering the quickness with which they are finished, the excellence of the work, if it be inspected, is admirable.——In all these
manufactures the sole of the foot is used, both by men and women,

as a work-board. They chop a piece of wood, or aught else upon it, even with an iron tool, without hurting themselves: it is indeed nearly as hard as the hoof of an ox.

Their method of procuring fire is this: They take a reed, and shave one side of the surface flat; in this they make a small incision to reach the pith, and introducing a stick, purposely blunted at the end, into it, turn it round between the hands (as chocolate is milled) as swiftly as possible, until flame be produced. As this operation is not only laborious, but the effect tedious, they frequently relieve each other at the exercise. And to avoid being often reduced to the necessity of putting it in practice, they always, if possible, carry a lighted stick with them, whether in their canoes or moving from place to place on land.

Their treatment of wounds must not be omitted. A doctor is with them, a person of importance and esteem; but his province seems rather to charm away occult diseases, than to act the surgeon's part, which, as a subordinate science, is exercised indiscriminately. Their excellent habit of body,* the effect of drinking water only, speedily heals wounds, without an exterior application which with us would take weeks or months to close. They are, nevertheless, sadly tormented by a cutaneous eruption; but we never found it contagious.—After receiving a contusion, if the part swell, they fasten a ligature very tightly above it, so as to stop all circulation. Whether to this application, or to their undebauched habit, it be attributable, I know not, but it is certain, that a disabled limb among them is rarely seen; although violent inflammations from bruises, which in us would bring on a gangrene, daily happen. If they get burned, either from rolling into the fire when asleep;

---

* Their native hardiness of constitution is great. I saw a woman, on the day she was brought to bed, carry her new-born infant from Botany Bay to Port Jackson, a distance of six miles; and afterwards light a fire and dress fish.

or from the flame catching the grass on which they lie, (both of which are common accidents) they cover the part with a thin paste of kneaded clay, which excludes the air, and adheres to the wound, until it be cured, and the eschar falls off.

Their form of government, and the detail of domestic life, yet remain untold. The former cannot occupy much space. Without distinctions of rank, except those which youth and vigour confer, theirs is strictly a system of *Equality*, attended with only one inconvenience—the strong triumph over the weak.—Whether any laws exist among them for the punishment of offences committed against society ; or whether the injured party in all cases seeks for relief in private revenge, I will not positively affirm ; though I am strongly inclined to believe, that only the latter method prevails. I have already said that they are divided into tribes ; but what constitutes the right of being enrolled in a tribe, or where exclusion begins and ends, I am ignorant. The tribe of Cameragal is of all the most numerous and powerful. Their superiority probably arose from possessing the best fishing ground ; and perhaps from their having suffered less from the ravages of the small-pox.

In the domestic detail their may be novelty, but variety is unattainable : one day must be very like another in the life of a savage. Summoned by the calls of hunger, and the returning light, he starts from his beloved indolence, and snatching up the remaining brand of his fire, hastens with his wife to the strand, to commence their daily task. In general the canoe is assigned to her, into which she puts the fire, and pushes off into deep water, to fish with hook and line, this being the province of the women. If she have a child at the breast, she takes it with her. And thus in her skiff, a piece of bark tied at both ends with vines, and the edge of it but just above the surface of the water, she pushes out regardless of the elements, if they be but commonly agitated. While she paddles to the fishing-bank, and while employed there, the child is placed on her shoulders, entwining its little legs around her neck, and closely grasping her hair with its hands. To its first cries she remains insensible, as she believes them to arise only from the inconveniency of a situation, to which she knows it must be inured. But if its plaints continue, and she supposes it to be in want of food, she ceases her fishing, and clasps it to her breast. An European spectator is struck with horror and astonishment, at their perilous situation : but accidents seldom happen. The management of the canoe alone appears a work of unsurmountable difficulty, its breadth is so inadequate to its length. The Indians, aware of its ticklish formation, practise from infancy to move in it without risk. Use only could reconcile them to the painful position in which they sit in it : they drop in the middle of the canoe upon their knees, and resting the buttocks on the heels, extend the knees to the sides, against which they press strongly, so as to form a poize, sufficient to retain the body in its situation, and relieve the weight which would otherwise fall wholly upon the toes. Either in this position, or cautiously moving in the centre of the vessel, the mother tends her child ; keeps up her fire, which is laid on a small patch of earth; paddles her boat ; broils fish ; and provides in part the subsistence of the day.—Their favourite bait for fish is a cockle.

The husband in the mean time warily moves to some rock, over which he can peep into unruffled water, to look for fish. For this purpose he always chuses a weather shore ; and the various windings of the numerous creeks and indents always afford one. Silent and watchful he chews a cockle, and spits it into the water. Allured by the bait, the fish appear from beneath the rock. He prepares his fish-gig, and pointing it downward, moves it gently towards the object, always trying to approach it as near as possible to the fish, before the stroke be given. At last he deems himself sufficiently advanced, and plunges it at his prey. If he has hit his mark, he continues his efforts and endeavours to transpierce it, or so to entangle the barbs in the flesh, as to prevent its escape. When he finds it secure he drops the instrument, and the fish, fastened on the prongs, rises to the surface, floated by the buoyancy of the staff. Nothing now remains to be done, but to haul it to him, with either a long stick, or another fish-gig (for an Indian, if he can help it, never goes into the water on these occasions) to disengage it, and to look out for fresh sport.

But sometimes the fish have either deserted the rocks for deeper water, or are too shy to suffer approach. He then launches his canoe, and leaving the shore behind, watches the rise of prey out of the water, and darts his gig at them to the distance of many yards. Large fish he seldom procures by this method; but among shoals of mullets, which are either pursued by enemies, or leap at objects on the surface, he is often successful. Baneelon has been seen to kill more than twenty fish by this method, in an afternoon. The women sometimes use the gig, and always carry one in each canoe, to strike large fish which may be hooked, and thereby facilitate the capture. But generally speaking, this instrument is appropriate to the men, who are never seen fishing with the line, and would indeed consider it as a degradation of their pre-eminence.

When prevented by tempestuous weather, or any other cause, from fishing, these people suffer severely. They have then no resource, but to pick up shell-fish, which may happen to cling to the rocks, and be cast on the beach; to hunt particular reptiles and small animals, which are scarce; to dig fern root in the swamps; or to gather a few berries, destitute of flavour and nutrition, which the woods afford. To alleviate the sensation of hunger, they tie a ligature tightly around the belly, as I have often seen our soldiers do from the same cause.

Let us, however, suppose them successful in procuring fish. The wife returns to land with her booty, and the husband quitting the rock joins his stock to hers; and they repair either to some neighbouring cavern, or to their hut. This last is composed of pieces of bark, very rudely piled together, in shape as like a soldier's tent as any known image to which I can compare it: too low to admit the lord of it to stand upright; but long and wide enough to admit three or four persons to lie under it. " Here shelters himself " a being, born with all those powers which education expands, " and all those sensations which culture refines." With a lighted stick brought from the canoe, they now kindle a small fire, at the mouth of the hut, and prepare to dress their meal. They begin by throwing the fish, exactly in the state in which it came from the water, on the fire. When it has become a little warmed they take it off, rub away the scales, and then peal off with their teeth the surface, which they find done, and eat. Now, and not before, they gut it; but if the fish be a mullet, or any other which has a fatty substance about the intestines, they carefully guard that part, and esteem it a delicacy. The cooking is now completed, by the remaining part being laid on the fire until it be sufficiently done. A bird, a lizard, a rat, or any other animal, they treat in the same manner: the feathers of the one, and the fur of the other, they thus get rid of.*

* They broil indiscriminately all substances which they eat. Though they boil water in small quantities, in oyster shells, for particular purposes, they never conceived it possible, until shewn by us, to dress meat by this method; having no vessel capable of containing a fish or a bird, which would stand fire.—Two of them once stole twelve pounds of rice, and carried it off. They knew how we cooked it; and by way of putting it in practice, they spread the rice on the ground, before a fire, and as it grew hot continued to throw water on it. Their ingenuity was however very ill rewarded; for the rice became so mingled with the dirt and sand on which it was laid, that even they could not eat it; and the whole was spoiled.

Unless summoned away by irresistable necessity, sleep always follows the repast. They would gladly prolong it until the following day; but the canoe wants repair; the fish-gig must be barbed afresh; new lines must be twisted, and new hooks chopped out—they depart to their respective tasks, which end only with the light.

Such is the general life of an Indian. But even he has his hours of relaxation, in seasons of success, when fish abounds. Wanton with plenty, he now meditates an attack upon the chastity of some neighbouring fair one; and watching his opportunity he seizes her, and drags her away to complete his purpose. The signal of war is lighted; her lover, her father, her brothers, her tribe, assemble, and vow revenge on the spoiler. He tells his story to his tribe: they judge the case to be a common one, and agree to support him. Battle ensues: they discharge their spears at each other, and legs and arms are transpierced. When the spears are expended the combatants close, and every species of violence is practiced: they seize their antagonist, and snap like enraged dogs: they wield the sword and club; the bone shatters beneath their fall; and they drop the prey of unsparing vengeance.

Too justly, as my observations teach me, has *Hobbes*, defined a state of nature, to be a state of war. In the method of waging it among these people, one thing should not, however, escape notice. Unlike all other Indians, they never carry on operations in the night, or seek to destroy by ambush and surprize. Their ardent fearless character, seeks fair and open combat only.

But enmity has its moments of pause: then they assemble to sing and dance. We always found their songs disagreeable, from their monotony: they are numerous, and vary both in measure and time. They have songs of war, of hunting, of fishing, for the rise and set of the sun, for rain, for thunder, and for many other occasions. One of these songs, which may be termed a speaking pantomime, recites the courtship between the sexes, and is accompanied with acting, highly expressive. I once heard and saw Nanbaree and Abaroo perform it: after a few preparatory motions, she gently sunk on the ground, as if in a fainting fit: Nanbaree applying his mouth to her ear, began to whisper in it; and baring her bosom, breathed on it several times. At length, the period of the swoon having expired, with returning animation she gradually raised herself: she now began to relate what she had seen in her vision, mentioning several of her countrymen by name, whom we knew to be dead; mixed with other strange incoherent matter, equally new and inexplicable, though all tending to one leading point—the sacrifice of her charms to her lover.

At their dances I have often been present; but I confess myself unable to convey in description, an accurate account of them. Like their songs, they are conceived to represent the progress of the passions, and the occupations of life. Full of seeming confusion, yet regular and systematic, their wild gesticulations, and frantic distortions of body, are calculated rather to terrify, than delight, a spectator. These dances consist of short parts, or acts, accompanied with frequent vociferations, and a kind of hissing, or whizzing noise: they commonly end with a loud rapid shout, and after a short respite are renewed. While the dance lasts, one of them (usually a person of note and estimation) beats time with a stick, on a wooden instrument, held in the left hand, accompanying the music with his voice; and the dancers sometimes sing in concert.—I have already mentioned that white is the colour appropriated to the dance; but the style of painting is left to every one's fancy. Some are streaked with waving lines from head to foot; others marked by broad crossbars, on the breast, back, and thighs; or encircled with spiral lines; or regularly striped like a zebra. Of these ornaments, the face never wants its share; and it is hard to conceive any thing in the shape of humanity, more hideous and terrific, than they appear to a stranger: seen, perhaps, through the livid gleam of a fire; the eyes surrounded by large white circles, in contrast with the black ground; the hair stuck full of pieces of bone; and in the hand a grasped club, which they occasionally brandish with the greatest fierceness and agility. Some dances are performed by men only; some by women only; and in others the sexes mingle. In one of them, I have seen the men drop on their hands and knees, and kiss the earth with the greatest fervor, between the kisses looking up to Heaven. They also frequently throw up their arms, exactly in the manner in which the dancers of the Friendly Islands are depicted, in one of the plates of Mr. Cook's last voyage.

Courtship here, as in other countries, is generally promoted by this exercise, where every one tries to recommend himself to attention and applause. Dancing not only proves an incentive, but offers an opportunity in its intervals. The first advances are made by the men, who strive to render themselves agreeable to their favourites, by presents of fishing-tackle, and other articles, which they know will prove acceptable. Generally speaking, a man has but one wife; but infidelity on the side of the husband, with the unmarried girls, is very frequent. For the most part, perhaps, they intermarry in their respective tribes: this rule is not, however, constantly observed; and there is reason to think, that a more than ordinary share of courtship and presents, on the part of the man, is required in this case. Such difficulty seldom operates to extinguish desire; and nothing is more common than for the unsuccessful suitor to ravish by force, that which he cannot accomplish by entreaty. I do not believe that very near connexions by blood, ever cohabit:—we knew of no instance of it.

But indeed the women are in all respects treated with savage barbarity ; condemned not only to carry the children, but all other burthens, they meet in return for submission only with blows, kicks, and every other mark of brutality. When an Indian is provoked by a woman, he either spears her, or knocks her down on the spot : on this occasion he always strikes on the head, using indiscriminately a hatchet, a club, or any other weapon, which may chance to be in his hand. The heads of the women are always consequently seen in the state which I found that of Gooree-deeana. Colbee, who was certainly, in other respects, a good tempered merry fellow, made no scruple of treating Daringa, who was a gentle creature, thus. Baneelon did the same to Barangaroo ; but she was a scold, and a vixen, and nobody pitied her. It must nevertheless be confessed, that the women often artfully study to irritate and inflame the passions of the men, although sensible that the consequence will alight on themselves.

Many a matrimonial scene of this sort have I witnessed. Lady Mary Wortley Montague, in her sprightly letters from Turkey, longs for some of the advocates for passive obedience and unconditional submission, then existing in England, to be present at the sights exhibited in a despotic government. A thousand times, in like manner, have I wished, that those European philosophers, whose closet speculations exalt a state of nature above a state of civilization, could survey the phantom, which their heated imaginations have raised : possibly they might then learn, that a state of nature is, of all others, least adapted to promote the happiness of a being, capable of sublime research, and unending ratiocination : that a savage roaming for prey amidst his native deserts, is a creature deformed by all those passions, which afflict and degrade our nature, unsoftened by the influence of religion, philosophy, and legal restriction : and that the more men unite their talents, the more closely the bands of society are drawn ; and civilization advanced, inasmuch is human felicity augmented, and man fitted for his unalienable station in the universe.

Of the language of New South Wales I once hoped to have sub-joined to this work such an exposition, as should have attracted public notice ; and have excited public esteem. But the abrupt departure of Mr. Dawes, who, stimulated equally by curiosity and philanthropy, had hardly set foot on his native country, when he again quitted it, to encounter new perils, in the service of the Sierra Leona company, precludes me from executing this part of my original intention, in which he had promised to co-operate with me; and in which he had advanced his researches beyond the reach of competition. The few remarks which I can offer shall be concisely detailed.

We were at first inclined to stigmatize this language as harsh and barbarous in its sounds ; their combinations of words, in the manner they utter them, frequently convey such an effect. But if not only their proper names of men and places, but many of their phrases, and a majority of their words, be simply and unconnect-edly considered, they will be found to abound with vowels, and to produce sounds sometimes mellifluous, and sometimes sonorous. What ear can object to the names of *Còlbee,* (pronounced exactly as Colby is with us) *Bèreewan, Bòndel, Im`eerawanyee, Deedòra, Wòlarawaree,* or *Bàneelon,* among the men; or to *Wereewèea, Gòoreedeeana, Mìlba,** or *Matìlba,* among the women. *Parramàtta, Gwèea, Càmeera, Càd-i, and Memel,* are names of places. The tribes derive their appellations from the places they inhabit: thus *Càmeeragal,* means the men who reside in the bay of Cameera; *Càdigal,* those who reside in the bay of Cadi; and so of the others. The women of the tribe are denoted by adding *eean* to any of the

* Mrs. Johnson, wife of the chaplain of the settlement, was so pleased with this name, that she christened her little girl, born in Port Jackson, Milba Maria Johnson.

D d

foregoing words: a *Cadigalèean* imports a woman living atCadi, or of the tribe of Cadigal. These words, as the reader will observe, are accented either on the first syllable or the penultima. In general, however, they are partial to the emphasis being laid as near the beginning of the word as possible.

Of compound words they seem fond: two very striking ones appear in the journal to the Hawkesbury. Their translations of our words into their language are always apposite, comprehensive, and drawn from images familiar to them: a gun, for instance, they call *Gooroobeera*, that is—*a stick of fire.*—Sometimes also, by a licence of language, they call those who carry guns by the same name. But the appellation by which they generally distinguished us was that of Bèreewolgal, meaning—*men come from afar.*—When they salute any one they call him Damèeli, or *namesake*, a term which not only implies courtesy and good-will, but a certain degree of affection in the speaker. An interchange of names with any one is also a symbol of friendship. Each person has several names; one of which, there is reason to believe, is always derived from the first fish or animal, which the child, in accompanying its father to the chace, or a fishing, may chance to kill.

Not only their combinations, but some of their simple sounds, were difficult of pronunciation to mouths purely English: diphthongs often occur: one of the most common is that of a e, or perhaps, a i, pronounced not unlike those letters in the French verb *baïr*, to hate. The letter y frequently follows d in the same syllable: thus the word which signifies a woman is *Dyin*; although the structure of our language requires us to spell it *Dee-in*.

But if they sometimes put us to difficulty, many of our words were to them unutterable. The letters s and v they never could pronounce: the latter became invariably w, and the former mocked all their efforts, which in the instance of Baneelon has been noticed; and a more unfortunate defect in learning our language could not easily be pointed out.

They use the ellipsis in speaking very freely; always omitting as many words as they possibly can, consistent with being understood. They inflect both their nouns and verbs regularly; and denote the cases of the former, and the tenses of the latter, not like the English by auxiliary words; but like the Latins by change of termination. Their nouns, whether substantive or adjective, seem to admit of no plural. I have heard Mr. Dawes hint his belief of their using a dual number, similar to the Greeks: but I confess that I never could remark aught to confirm it. The method by which they answer a question, that they cannot resolve, is similar to what we sometimes use. Let for example the following question be put—*Waw Colbee yagoono?*—Where is Colbee to-day?—Waw, *baw!*—Where, *indeed!* would be the reply. They use a direct and positive negative: but express the affirmative by a nod of the head, or an inclination of the body.

Opinions have greatly differed, whether or not, their language be copious. In one particular it is notoriously defective; they cannot count with precision more than *four*. However as far as ten, by holding up the fingers, they can both comprehend others, and explain themselves. Beyond four every number is called great; and should it happen to be very large, *great great*, which is an Italian idiom also. This occasions their computations of time and space to be very confused and incorrect: of the former they have no measure but the visible diurnal motion of the sun, or the monthly revolution of the moon.

To conclude the history of a people for whom I cannot but feel some share of affection: let those who have been born in more favoured lands, and who have profited by more enlightened systems, compassionate, but not despise, their destitute and obscure situation. Children of the same omniscient paternal care, let them recollect, that by the fortuitous advantage of birth alone, they possess superiority: that untaught, unaccommodated man, is the same in Pall-Mall, as in the wilderness of New South Wales: and ultimately let them hope, and trust, that the progress of reason, and the splendor of revelation, will in their proper and allotted season, be permitted to illumine, and transfuse into these desert regions, knowledge, virtue, and happiness.

CHAPTER XVIII.

Observations on the Convicts.

A short account of that class of men for whose disposal and advantage the colony was principally, if not totally, founded, seems necessary.

If it be recollected how large a body of these people are now congregated, in the settlement of Port Jackson, and at Norfolk Island, it will, I think, not only excite surprize, but afford satisfaction, to learn, that in a period of four years few crimes of a deep dye, or of a hardened nature have been perpetrated: murder and unnatural sins rank not hitherto in the catalogue of their enormities: and one suicide only has been committed.

To the honour of the female part of our community let it be recorded, that only one woman has suffered capital punishment: on her condemnation she pleaded pregnancy; and a jury of venerable matrons was impanneled on the spot, to examine and pronounce her state ; which the forewoman, a grave personage between 60 and 70 years old, did, by this short address to the court; 'Gentlemen! 'she is as much with child as I am.' Sentence was accordingly passed, and she was executed.

Besides the instance of Irving, two other male convicts, William Bloodsworth, of Kingston upon Thames, and John Arscott, of Truro, in Cornwall, were both emancipated, for their good conduct, in the years 1790 and 1791. Several men whose terms of transportation had expired, and against whom no legal impediment existed to prevent their departure, have been permitted to enter in merchant ships wanting hands : and, as my Rose Hill journals testify, many others have had grants of land assigned to them, and are become settlers in the country.

In so numerous a community many persons of perverted genius, and of mechanical ingenuity, could not but be assembled. Let me produce the following example:—Frazer was an iron manufacturer, bred at Sheffield, of whose abilities, as a workman, we had witnessed many proofs. The governor had written to England for a set of locks, to be sent out for the security of the public stores, which were to be so constructed as to be incapable of being picked. On their arrival his excellency sent for Frazer, and bade him examine them; telling him at the same time that they could not be picked. Frazer laughed, and asked for a crooked nail only, to open them all. A nail was brought, and in an instant he verified his assertion. Astonished at his dexterity, a gentleman present determined to put it to farther proof. He was sent for in a hurry, some days after, to the hospital, where a lock of still superior intricacy and expence to the others had been provided. He was told that the key was lost, and that the lock must be immediately picked. He examined it attentively ; remarked that it was the production of a workman ; and demanded ten minutes to make an instrument ' *to speak with it.*' Without carrying the lock with him, he went directly to his shop; and at the expiration of his term returned, applied his instrument, and open flew the lock. But it was not only in this part of his business that he excelled : he executed every branch of it in superior style. Had not his villainy been still more notorious than his skill, he would have proved an invaluable possession to a new country. He had passed through innumerable scenes in life, and had played many parts. When too lazy to work at his trade, he had turned thief in fifty different shapes; was a receiver of stolen goods ; a soldier ; and a travelling conjurer. He once confessed to me, that he had made a set of tools, for a gang of coiners, every man of whom was hanged.

Were the nature of the subject worthy of farther illustration, many similar proofs of misapplied talents, might be adduced.

Their love of the marvellous, has been recorded in an early part of this work. The imposture of the gold finder, however prominent and glaring, nevertheless contributed to awaken attention, and to create merriment. He enjoyed the reputation of a discoverer, until experiment detected the imposition. But others were less successful to acquire even momentary admiration. The execution of forgery seems to demand at least neatness of imitation, and dexterity of address.—On the arrival of the first fleet of ships from England, several convicts brought out recommendatory letters, from different friends. Of these some were genuine, and many owed their birth to the ingenuity of the bearers. But these last were all such bungling performances, as to produce only instant detection, and succeeding contempt. One of them addressed to the governor, with the name of Baron Hotham affixed to it, began " Honored Sir!"

A leading distinction, which marked the convicts on their outset in the colony, was an use of what is called the *flash*, or *kiddy* language. In some of our early courts of justice, an interpreter was frequently necessary to translate the deposition of the witness, and the defence of the prisoner. This language has many dialects. The sly dexterity of the pickpocket ; the brutal ferocity of the footpad ; the more elevated career of the highwayman ; and the deadly purpose of the midnight ruffian, is each strictly appropriate in the terms which distinguish and characterize it. I have ever been of opinion, that an abolition of this unnatural jargon would open the path to reformation. And my observations on these people have constantly instructed me, that indulgence in this infatuating cant, is more deeply associated with depravity, and continuance in vice, than is generally supposed. I recollect hardly one instance of a return to honest pursuits, and habits of industry, where this miserable perversion of our noblest and peculiar faculty was not previously conquered.

Those persons to whom the inspection and management of our numerous and extensive prisons in England are committed, will perform a service to society, by attending to the foregoing observation. Let us always keep in view, that punishment, when not directed to promote reformation, is arbitrary, and unauthorized.

CHAPTER XIX.

Facts relating to the Probability of establishing a Whale Fishery on the Coast of New South Wales :—With Thoughts on the same.

In every former part of this publication, I have studiously avoided mentioning a whale fishery; as the information relating to it will, I conceive, be more acceptably received in this form, by those to whom it is addressed, than if mingled with other matter.

Previous to entering on this detail, it must be observed, that several of the last fleet of ships which had arrived from England, with convicts, were fitted out with implements for whale fishing, and were intended to sail for the coast of Brazil, to pursue the fishery, immediately on having landed the convicts.

On the 14th of October, 1791, the Britannia, captain Melville, one of these ships, arrived at Sydney. In her passage between Van Dieman's Land and Port Jackson, the master reported, that he had seen a large shoal of spermaceti whales. His words were, " I saw more whales, at one time, around my ship, than in the " whole of six years, which I have fished on the coast of Brazil."

This intelligence was no sooner communicated, than all the whalers were eager to push to sea: Melville himself was among the most early ; and on the 10th of November, returned to Port Jackson, more confident of success than before. He assured me, that in the fourteen days which he had been out, he had seen more sper-

E e

maceti whales, than in all his former life : they amounted he said
to many thousands, most of them of enormous magnitude; and
had he not met with bad weather, he could have killed as many
as he pleased. Seven he did kill ; but, owing to the stormy agitated state of the water, he could not get any of them aboard. In
one however, which in a momentary interval of calm, was killed
and secured, by a ship in company, he shared. The oil and *head
matter* of this fish, he extolled as of an extraordinary fine quality.
He was of opinion the former would fetch ten pounds per ton more
in London, than that procured on the Brazil coast. He had not
gone farther south than 37°; and described the latitude of 35° to be
the place where the whales most abounded, just on the edge of sound-
ings, which here extends about fifteen leagues from the shore ;
though perhaps, on other parts of the coast, the bank will be found
to run hardly so far off.

On the following day (November 11th) the Mary Anne, captain Munro, another of the whalers, returned into port, after having been out sixteen days. She had gone as far south as 41°; but
saw not a whale ; and had met with tremendously bad weather, in
which she had shipped a sea, that had set her boiling coppers afloat,
and had nearly carried them overboard.

November 22d. The William and Anne, captain Buncker, returned, after having been more than three weeks out, and putting
into Broken Bay. This is the ship that had killed the fish in
which Melville shared. Buncker had met with no farther success,
owing, he said, entirely, to gales of wind ; for he had seen several
immense shoals ; and was of opinion, that he should have secured
fifty tons of oil, had the weather been tolerably moderate. I asked him whether he thought the whales he had seen were fish of
passage. " No," he answered, " they were going on every point of
" the compass, and were evidently on feeding ground, which I saw

" no reason to doubt that they frequent." Melville afterwards
confirmed to me this observation.—December 3d, the Mary Anne
and Matilda again returned. The former had gone to the southward, and off Port Jervis had fallen in with two shoals of whales,
nine of which were killed : but, owing to bad weather, part of five
only were got on board: as much, the master computed, as would
yield 30 barrels of oil. He said the whales were the least shy of any
he had ever seen ; "not having been cut up" (a fisherman's phrase
for harrassed, disturbed.) The latter had gone to the northward,
and had seen no whales, but a few fin-backs.

On the 5th of December, both these ships sailed again ; and on
the 16th and 17th of the month (just before the author sailed for
England) they, and the Britannia, and William and Anne, returned
to Port Jackson, without success; having experienced a continua-
tion of the bad weather ; and seen very few fish. They all said
that their intention was to give the coast one more trial ; and if it
miscarried to quit it and steer to the northward in search of less
tempestuous seas.

The only remark which I have to offer to adventurers, on the
above subject, is not to suffer discouragement, by concluding that
bad weather only is to be found on the coast of New South Wales,
where the whales have hitherto been seen. Tempests happen
sometimes there, as in other seas: but let them feel assured, that
there are in every month of the year many days, in which the
whale fishery may be safely carried on. The evidence of the
abundance in which spermaceti whales are sometimes seen, is in-
controvertible: that which speaks to their being *not fish of passage*,
is at least respectable, and hitherto uncontradicted. The prospect
merits attention—may it stimulate to enterprize.

The two discoveries of Port Jervis and Matilda Bay (which are
to be found in the foregoing sheets) may yet be wanting in the maps

of the coast. My account of their geographic situation, except possibly in the exact longitude of the latter, (a point not very material) may be safely depended upon. A knowledge of Oyster Bay, discovered and laid down by the Mercury store-ship, in the year 1789, would also be desirable: but this I am incapable of furnishing.

Here terminates my subject. Content with the humble province of detailing facts, and connecting events by undisturbed narration, I leave to others the task of anticipating glorious, or gloomy, consequences, from the establishment of a colony, which unquestionably demands serious investigation, ere either its prosecution, or abandonment, be determined.

But doubtless not only those who planned, but those who have been delegated to execute, an enterprize of such magnitude, have deeply revolved, that " great national expence does not imply the " necessity of national suffering. While revenue is employed " with success to some valuable end, the profits of every adventure " being more than sufficient to repay its costs, the public should " gain, and its resources should continue to multiply. But an " expence whether sustained at home or abroad; whether a waste " of the present, or an anticipation of the future, revenue, if it " bring no adequate return, is to be reckoned among the causes of " national ruin." *

* Ferguson's Essay on the History of Civil Society.

THE END.

For EU product safety concerns, contact us at Calle de José Abascal, 56–1°, 28003 Madrid, Spain or eugpsr@cambridge.org.

www.ingramcontent.com/pod-product-compliance
Ingram Content Group UK Ltd.
Pitfield, Milton Keynes, MK11 3LW, UK
UKHW030901150625
459647UK00021B/2691